HOW TO RESTORE

Gearboxes and Axles

OSPREY
RESTORATION
GUIDE 13

HOW TO RESTORE
Gearboxes and Axles

Ivor Carroll /
Matthew Greenshields B.Sc.

Published in 1987 by Osprey Publishing Limited
59 Grosvenor Street, London W1X 9DA
Reprinted spring 1989

Sole distributors for the USA

Publishers & Wholesalers Inc
Osceola, Wisconsin 54020, USA

British Library Cataloguing in Publication Data

Carroll, Ivor
  How to restore gearboxes and axles.—
  (Osprey restoration guide; 13)
  1. Automobiles—Maintenance and repair
  I. Title
  629.28'722   TL152
  ISBN 0-85045-731-9

Editor Tony Thacker

Filmset by Tameside Filmsetting Ltd,
Ashton-under-Lyne, Lancashire

Printed by BAS Printers Ltd, Over Wallop,
Hampshire, Great Britain

CONTENTS

	Introduction	7
1	Transmission principles	11
2	Transmission layouts	31
3	Clutches	53
4	Gearbox overhaul	68
5	Final drives and differentials	94
6	Propshaft, driveshafts and joints	105
7	Gearchanges and linkages	118
	Troubleshooter	123
	Index	127

Introduction

With *How to Restore Gearboxes and Axles* it is our intention to give you a comprehensive insight into the workings of a car's transmission, and by *transmission* we mean the entire driveline from the end of the engine crankshaft to the driven wheels, rather than just the gearbox unit itself. We do not deal with the overhaul of automatic transmissions due to the relative complexity of epicyclic gear trains and hydraulic command mechanisms, notwithstanding the greater need for specialized tooling and test equipment. Nor do we systematically proceed through the complete overhaul of one particular transmission, as so many different varieties are to be found on manual gearbox cars from the 1950s to the present day (the period in time that our advice on transmission restoration will mostly cover).

What we are concerned with, however, is a brief explanation of the various components which are found in a vehicle's drivelines, the principles involved in transmitting drive, the typical methods of dismantling and assembly of units and, probably most importantly, the means by which to assess the condition and serviceability of the individual components of the drivetrain.

Anyone tackling a gearbox overhaul for the first time is faced with a daunting task; indeed, an experienced motor technician facing the strip-down of a gearbox which he has never previously worked on faces a similarly daunting task, for every gearbox, although doing the same job as another, is different in construction. For this reason we would advise even the more experienced transmission man to equip himself with a workshop manual for the type of car concerned when undertaking a rebuild, for, even if you understand everything that you see, there may well be hidden fastenings and obscure tricks involved which can stump an expert. We have used Autodata car repair manuals as a handy source of reference for this book, and many of the line drawings included are reproduced from them. These manuals are simply worded, clearly illustrated and, of course, specific to each car, and we can therefore recommend that they be used in conjunction with *How to Restore Gearboxes and Axles*. In addition to Autodata Ltd, we should like to thank the following for the use of their illustrations: Hutchinson & Co. Ltd

(Publishers), Hillier & Pittuck, Ford Motor Co. Ltd, Peugeot Société Anonyme, Austin Rover Group Ltd, Automotive Products PLC, Regie Nationale Des Usines Renault, Alfa Romeo SpA, V.A.G. Ltd and Jaguar Cars Ltd.

Different gearboxes from one motor manufacturer invariably look similar internally, as the same design of synchromesh is usually applied throughout the range, and often identical selectors and interlock devices too. Thus Ford manual gearboxes, of which there are about five basic types, share very similar dismantling and reassembly techniques, as the same fixings, fastenings and mainshaft design are used throughout. Someone overhauling a Peugeot gearbox, though, will find quite radically different looking internals and a whole new set of rules for pulling apart and putting back together again. In many cases a host of special tooling is recommended for the stripping of a gearbox and although some of these tools are highly specialized and actually *vital* for the job, many others are not totally necessary and can be improvised. A basic tool kit is the obvious starting point and we will qualify what comprises a 'basic' kit later.

Probably the greatest potential problem area, from the home mechanic's point of view, concerns interference fits where one component is secured to another either by first heating it up and then letting it cool and therefore shrink down on to the first, or else by pressing it on to the other by means of a hydraulic press. Where components are so mated it is vital that you have a specific workshop manual by your side to warn you of the fact and also to inform you of the best means of separation of the parts concerned. Where a hydraulic press is not available or a hot oil bath is impractical, you will invariably find local engineering works will be pleased to carry out such minor (to them anyway!) tasks on the assemblies you supply for a nominal fee, so even the greatest apparent difficulties need not be insurmountable.

Bearing in mind that manual gearboxes, no matter how they are designed and constructed, all do the same job, they also suffer from the same afflictions, the most common of which are: oil leaks, grating or crunching gears, whining in

A selection of tools often vital to transmission overhaul

any number of gears and jumping out of gear. Less commonly a manual gearbox can suffer from stiff or sloppy gearchange, loss of any number of gears or complete failure due to internal breakage. Grating gears are a great favourite and are usually due to ineffective synchromesh caused by wear of the synchronizers or weak selector detents, although an external cause of this problem can be a worn or badly adjusted clutch overloading the synchromesh units to the point where they cannot function as intended. Correct operation of the clutch is therefore

External, internal and 'horseshoe' circlip pliers

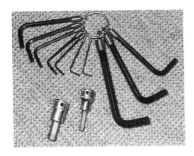

Above **Allen keys and hex socket adaptors**

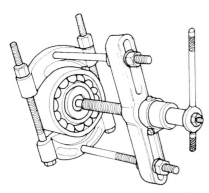

Above **A universal bearing puller in use to remove a ball-race bearing from a shaft**

vital to good gearbox operation so we will discuss clutches in greater detail in a later chapter, just as we will treat the remaining items in the driveline—propshaft, differential, transfer gears, driveshafts and axles—in their own chapters. Quick diagnosis of most transmission problems is possible with the aid of the 'Troubleshooter' which is included as the last chapter of the book.

As previously mentioned, you *must* have certain basic tools before commencing any work, as otherwise frustration and defeat will certainly end up being the order of the day. Our recommendation for a basic tool kit is as follows: fine-nosed pliers, snub-nosed pliers, self-locking grips, non-locking grips, large and small adjustable spanners, combination (ring and open-end) spanners—Imperial or Metric depending on car type, $\frac{3}{8}$ in. drive socket set—again Imperial or Metric, $\frac{1}{2}$ in. socket set—again Imperial or Metric, low-range and high-range torque wrenches, screwdrivers of all types and sizes, steel rule, rawhide mallet, ball pein hammer, centre punch, various brass and wood drifts, various grades of wet-and-dry paper, various containers of differing sizes for collecting stripped components, cleaning tank or basin with a suitable cleaning solvent (paraffin or water-soluble cleaner, e.g. Gunk).

The addition of the following items is often vital to transmission overhaul: internal and external circlip pliers (for conventional circlips with external 'eyes'), flat-ended circlip pliers for eyeless 'horseshoe' and 'ear' type circlips, various pin punches, a selection of Allen keys—Imperial or Metric—and/or hex socket adaptors, general gear/sprocket puller, universal bearing puller, feeler gauges, clutch alignment mandrel—see chapter 3, piston ring compressing clamp—see chapter 4, long-reach magnet, cold chisels—note that these should only be used to assist in removing components that are to be discarded, such as a speedometer drive gear.

Autodata Limited are at St. Peter's Road, Maidenhead, Berkshire SL6 7QU, England.

Chapter 1 | Transmission principles

Torque and speed

Torque is defined as the turning effect of a force applied at a distance from and perpendicular to a centre of rotation and it is the engine torque which we wish to take from the crankshaft to the driven wheels. To better describe what torque is we can imagine someone attempting to loosen a tight bolt with a spanner; if he uses a short spanner it doesn't give him enough leverage to overcome the friction that is holding that bolt stationary. If, however, he tries longer and longer spanners he will eventually reach a point where the torque applied to the bolt is sufficient to overcome the friction and rotate it.

So where has this extra torque come from? Clearly not from an inert spanner but from the fact that by increasing the distance between his hand and the bolt our mechanic has traded in a large amount of applied force and a short distance of hand travel against less applied force but greater travel. So if he fully unscrews the bolt using a 10-inch spanner his hand will travel twice the distance in circles than if he undid it using a 5-inch spanner and hence do the same amount of work, but he will only have to apply half as much force. This explains why torque is measured in pounds feet or kilogramme metres, for such units show the multiplicative relationship between how much force is being applied and at what distance away from the centre of rotation it is being applied.

So why have a gearbox?

The internal combustion engine can only produce so much torque and if that amount of torque is insufficient to overcome resistance to the car's forward motion, such as hills, headwinds and overweight grannies in the back seat, then it must have a means by which it can increase its rotational speed in relation to the car's road speed so that it can always deliver enough torque to maintain motion. If the car has a four-speed gearbox then maximum torque will be available in first gear to drive the wheels but the resultant road speed per thousand rpm of the engine will be far less than in fourth gear, where considerably less torque will be available to drive the wheels. Thus the gearbox allows a trade-off of torque at the driven wheels against vehicle velocity. The speed reduction ratio of a pair of gears is simply calculated by dividing the number of teeth on the driven gear wheel by the number of teeth on the driving gear wheel.

If your car were not equipped with a gearbox then the following situations would be apparent:

Firstly, the car would have very poor acceleration from a standstill and the clutch would have to be ridden (slipped) for quite a time so as to avoid engine stalling. In fact it would have to be slipped until a reasonable road speed had been reached—anything between 10 and 20 mph—before it could be fully engaged to give direct drive, and even then there would be so little torque at the driven wheels that it could easily be stalled and would barely accelerate. Should the car then meet a hill and commence an upward climb, the gradient resistance would ensure that the engine speed would drop again to a point where the engine would stall. And, of course, there would also be the impracticality of not being able to drive the car at any speed less than the 10- or 20-odd mph without slipping the clutch, nor of being able to reverse it for that matter!

Overdrive and final drive

So what exactly is meant by 'overdrive'? If you imagine, purely for the sake of argument, that drive is taken directly from the crankshaft to the gearbox output shaft (and thence the propshaft on a rear-wheel-drive car) without any ratio changes via gears, then the propshaft will rotate at exactly the same speed as the crankshaft at all times; this is direct drive, or a drive ratio of 1:1, and it is usually the ratio chosen for the top gear of a three- or four-speed gearbox.

If, however, by means of gearing, you can arrange for every revolution of the gearbox output shaft/propshaft to correspond to anything less than one revolution of the crankshaft, you then have stepped-up gearing or *overdrive*. Overdrive is desirable for fast continuous driving such as on motorway journeys as it allows the engine to turn more slowly for a given road speed than it would if transmission were by direct drive, thereby allowing quieter running, lessened fuel consumption and reduced engine wear. A typical overdrive ratio is 0.7:1, where the gearbox output shaft/propshaft turns one revolution for every $\frac{7}{10}$ of a revolution of the crankshaft. Overdrive on a car can either be in the form of an electrically and hydraulically selected epicyclic gear ratio between gearbox output and propshaft, or else (and more commonly these days) a fifth gearset in a conventionally designed manual gearbox (fifth gear).

Because of the high speeds at which the internal combustion automobile engine runs, there has to be a reduction gear between the gearbox output shaft/propshaft and the driven wheels to allow the wheels to turn at a considerably slower speed than the crankshaft. This is known as the *final drive*, where the driving gear is referred to as the *pinion* and the driven gear the *crown wheel*. It would be ridiculous to have a car which at an engine speed of 1500 rpm in top gear was also spinning its road wheels at 1500 rpm, so this final reduction ratio is required to allow the high-speed internal combustion engine to run at speeds much higher than the car's wheels. A typical final-drive reduction ratio is 3.5:1, which means that in direct-drive gear the driven wheels are rotating three and a half times slower than the gearbox output shaft/propshaft. The final drive and *differential* are one assembly, the differential components being mounted to the crown wheel on the same axis as the car's axle shafts.

More ratios

As we have seen, the more torque an engine produces in relation to the weight of the car, the fewer gears it needs for good acceleration, and the higher the top gear ratio can be (whether that be a third, fourth or fifth gear). But of course the more ratios there are, the closer those ratios can afford to be, which means that the engine speed will drop less for each upward gearchange and stay closer to its maximum torque or most economic operating speed. If, for fast acceleration, you change up into the next gear at a point in the rev range which will result in the engine then running at such a speed that it is producing more or less its maximum torque (typically at 2500 to 3500 rpm), then the acceleration in the new gear will be greatest, which may be desirable. But, if you are to have a reasonably high (relaxed) top gear and a sufficiently low first gear to enable the car to pull away fully laden from a standstill up a steep hill and you only have three ratios, then each of the three ratios will be considerably different from the others (widely spaced) and so acceleration will suffer, because each time a higher gear is selected the engine-speed drop will be greater and the engine will produce less than peak torque in the higher gear; thus more gears are beneficial both to performance and economy.

The clutch
What role, then, does the clutch play in the transmission system? In every car there is a need for a disconnection in drive between the engine and the transmission/road wheels when the car is brought to a halt as, unlike an electric motor, the internal combustion engine cannot provide torque from a standstill, and so will stall rather clumsily if dragged down to very low speeds by the transmission. The clutch acts as a variable connection between the two and also allows progressive transmission of torque from one to the other so that smooth pull-away can be achieved. This disconnection between power unit and gearbox is also needed for reliable and fuss-free gear selection.

The two duties of smooth drive take-up and complete disengagement can be performed by various mechanisms, and the dry friction system is considered to be one of the most effective and efficient.

In brief, the operation of a friction clutch (Fig. 1.1), is effected by these basic components: the engine's flywheel, an asbestos friction plate and a pressure plate which is connected to a circular spring-steel diaphragm or a ring of coil springs. Normally the friction plate is clamped firmly between flywheel and pressure plate by the action of the spring or springs, and the centre hub of the friction plate is permanently engaged to the input shaft of the gearbox. In this state, all rotation of the crankshaft/flywheel is transmitted to the gearbox input shaft. The friction between flywheel, friction plate (clutch plate) and pressure plate, is proportional to the clamping force exerted by the spring(s), and so by opposing this force, the friction, and thus the rotational drive, can be progressively reduced until there is none transmitted to the gearbox input shaft and the vehicle will not move.

Driving the wheels

So, tracing the transmission driveline through from the crankshaft, we so far have: clutch, gearbox and final drive. In our chapter on transmission layouts we will discuss the many alternative arrangements for drivetrains which are currently used and which are determined mostly by the location of the engine in the car (i.e. front, rear or central), which wheels are driven and the direction in which the engine points. For the moment though, returning to the conventional transmission layout which is front engine (inline or north–south) and rear drive, the driveline is completed by the driveshafts or axle shafts which take the

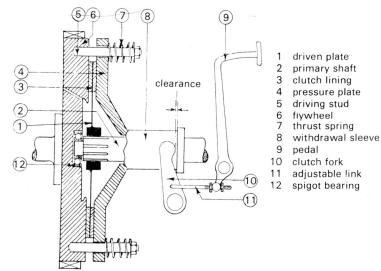

clearance

1   driven plate
2   primary shaft
3   clutch lining
4   pressure plate
5   driving stud
6   flywheel
7   thrust spring
8   withdrawal sleeve
9   pedal
10 clutch fork
11 adjustable link
12 spigot bearing

Fig. 1.1. A cross-section through a simplified single-plate friction clutch using coil springs

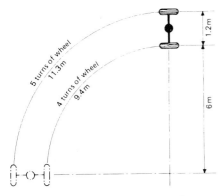

Fig. 1.2. This illustration shows the different distances travelled by inner and outer wheels when turning a corner. The difference in turning radii in this case between inner and outer wheels is 1.2 m—the track width of the axle

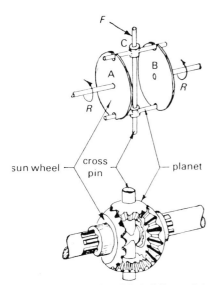

Fig. 1.3. A simplified differential

power from the final drive and transmit it to each of the rear road wheels. Whether they be open driveshafts with flexible joints to accommodate suspension movement, or axle shafts enclosed in the rigid axle casing and supported by bearings at either end of the casing, they fulfil the purpose of transmitting torque to the wheels. The choice of shaft depends on the suspension type and is not dictated by the transmission design.

Differential action

In the process of passing drive from propshaft or gearbox output shaft to axle shafts, a *differential* action has to be provided to allow for the different turning speeds of the two driven wheels when the car negotiates anything other than a straight path on the road. Because the inner and outer wheels describe curves of different radii as the car is cornered, one travels further than the other and thus turns faster (Fig. 1.2). If both were forced to rotate at the same rate by a fixed axle then the result would be that slip would occur between the tyres and the road surface, resulting in excessive tyre wear. Thus the differential (which forms one and the same assembly as the final drive mentioned earlier) does exactly as its name implies and allows a speed differential between the driven wheels.

The differential action is achieved by securing a 'sun' gear at the driven end of each axle shaft as shown in Fig. 1.3, both of which are driven by 'planet' gears rotating with the crown wheel. The crown wheel is usually a helical bevel gear positioned perpendicular to the propshaft and driven around by the propshaft by means of a helical pinion (Fig. 1.4). This gearset is known as the *final drive*. The two planet gears are mounted on a 'planet pin' which is fixed to the differential *cage* and always turns with the crown wheel. So drive is applied to the planet pin via the crown wheel; the pin in turn drives the planet gears, exerting an equal torque on each sun gear irrespective of their speed. When the car turns a bend, however, one wheel slows down and causes the planet gears to rotate on the planet pin to speed up the outer wheel. Straight-line motoring allows the entire assembly to rotate at the same speed.

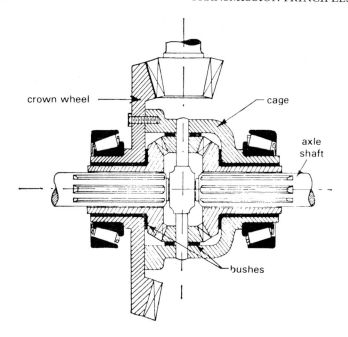

crown wheel

cage

axle shaft

bushes

Fig. 1.4. Cross-section through the final drive and differential. This is a bevel-type final drive as used in a rear-wheel-drive car or any automobile with an inline gearbox

The sliding-mesh gearbox—operation

The simple sliding-mesh manual gearbox, which formed the basis of today's more sophisticated synchromesh gearbox, is a good starting point for describing the operation of gearboxes in general (Fig. 1.5). It comprises the mainshaft and layshaft running parallel to each other, the former carrying the driving gears (one less than there are ratios) which can slide on it by virtue of splines but which are in permanent rotational mesh with it. The layshaft is usually one casting which incorporates the corresponding driven gears which cannot slide or rotate independently of each other.

Drive from the clutch is transmitted to the gearbox by a short input shaft (at the other end of which is the clutch plate) which is coaxial with the mainshaft but not connected to it. It carries a spur gear which is permanently meshed with the front layshaft gear and thus the input shaft and layshaft spin continually when the clutch is engaged. The gear wheels, which are splined to the mainshaft, carry grooved sleeves on their ends which have free-running selector forks located in them to allow the

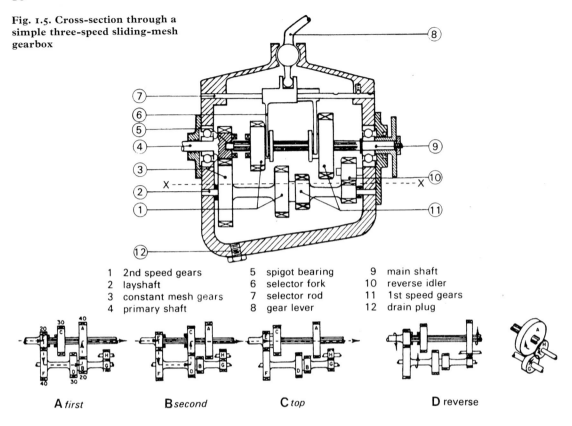

Fig. 1.5. Cross-section through a simple three-speed sliding-mesh gearbox

1	2nd speed gears	5	spigot bearing	9	main shaft
2	layshaft	6	selector fork	10	reverse idler
3	constant mesh gears	7	selector rod	11	1st speed gears
4	primary shaft	8	gear lever	12	drain plug

A *first*   B *second*   C *top*   D *reverse*

gear wheels to be slid along the shaft splines by the selector mechanism and gear lever.

By this means the mainshaft gear wheels can be individually engaged with their corresponding gear wheels on the layshaft, but, when the gearbox is in *neutral*, all mainshaft gear wheels are positioned so that they do not touch the layshaft gears. In this way the layshaft spins but the mainshaft remains stationary and, as the car's propshaft is connected to the rear end of the mainshaft, there is no torque transmitted to the road wheels. However, by moving the gear lever into first-gear position, the first-gear gear wheel is slid forward to engage with its layshaft gear wheel and all other gears are positioned in neutral (A, Fig. 1.5). In this gear the reduced layshaft speed (relative to crankshaft speed), which is caused by the constant-mesh gears mentioned previously, is further reduced by the ratio of the first-gear main and layshaft gear wheels. In selecting second gear, the second mainshaft gear wheel is slid back to engage with its corresponding layshaft gear wheel and this same gear lever movement disengages the mesh of the first-gear gear wheel set (B, Fig. 1.5). The driving gear wheel is larger in diameter than that of the first gearset and the driven gear wheel is smaller in diameter than that of the first gearset. Thus the reduction ratio is less and the difference between propshaft and crankshaft speeds is less.

In third gear (which was typically top gear in the sliding-mesh gearbox), direct drive is used for reasons of efficiency and is achieved by locking the front mainshaft gear wheel to the input shaft so that clutch plate, input shaft, mainshaft and propshaft all move together as one (C, Fig. 1.5). Of course, the layshaft, which is in constant mesh with the input shaft gear wheel, also spins but drives nothing.

Reverse gear

Reversing the direction of the output torque at the mainshaft is a simple matter of moving the first-gear mainshaft gear wheel into an alternative position whereby it meshes with an idler gear (idler because it is not driven and it drives nothing, but merely spins on a short length of fixed shaft), which in turn is in permanent mesh with another layshaft gear (D, Fig. 1.5). The idler naturally turns in the opposite direction to the layshaft gear which drives it, and so when the mainshaft first gear is introduced into mesh with it, the direction of mainshaft rotation is reversed to that of the layshaft; thus the propshaft turns in the opposite direction and the car reverses. This method of obtaining reverse gear is still the common method today. Fig. 1.6 shows a Ford gearbox with the reverse idler gear in mesh with its layshaft counterpart.

The need for synchronization—double-declutching

It is obvious that when changing gear with this type of arrangement, the two gears to be meshed cannot simply be pushed together into engagement as they would be rotating at different speeds and would, despite the bevelled ends to

Fig. 1.6. View inside a Ford inline gearbox with the mainshaft removed. The straight-cut reverse-gear idler wheel is shown in mesh with its layshaft counter-gear

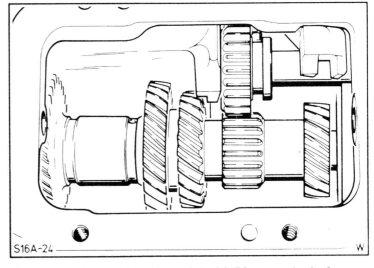

the gears, reject each other or 'clash'. If one mainshaft gear, running at a speed determined by the layshaft (and so the engine) and its own diameter, is suddenly disengaged and a new mainshaft gear of a different diameter is made to engage with the layshaft, the mainshaft itself, which continues to turn at the same speed, will need to alter its speed by the amount dictated by the difference in ratios before clash-free mesh can be achieved. The mainshaft speed cannot be altered without changing the *car's* velocity so the *layshaft* speed must be changed instead. If the newly selected gear is of a higher ratio than the previous one (i.e. fourth is selected after third) then the layshaft speed will have to *decrease*; if a lower ratio is being selected (i.e. second after third) then its speed must *increase* to synchronize it with the speed that the new ratio dictates.

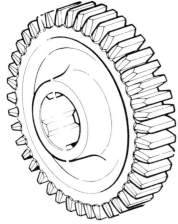

Fig. 1.7. A straight-cut gear wheel. Note the pointed bevels at the end of each tooth—these assist mesh when the two gears to be meshed are not in perfect alignment

This can be accomplished by the driver, who can increase the speed of the layshaft by means of the engine (via the throttle and with the clutch disengaged) or decrease it by briefly selecting neutral so that the engine's own inertia (its normal resistance to movement) decelerates it prior to selecting the new gear. Thus when 'changing up' you depress the clutch pedal, select neutral, release the clutch pedal and immediately depress it again before pushing the lever into gear. When 'changing down', however, it is necessary to depress the clutch pedal, select neutral, release the clutch pedal, dab the throttle pedal to instantly raise the engine revs by the required amount and then depress the clutch again and select the new gear when it is judged that the speeds are matched. For both up- and down-changes, the judgement of speed matching is effected very much by 'feel', which is why 'double-declutching'—as this operation is known—needs practise to perfect.

Constant-mesh gearbox

The need for a system which could automatically synchronize gear engagements became evident and the first step towards the synchromesh gearbox was the un-synchronized *constant-mesh* gearbox, which is similar in layout. The term 'constant-mesh' is pretty well self-explanatory, for with this type the mainshaft gear wheels are in permanent mesh with their corresponding layshaft gear wheels and are mounted on bronze bushes or needle roller bearings, free to rotate on the mainshaft until locked to it by an external means effected by the driver (Fig. 1.8).

With the engine running and the gearbox in the neutral position, all the gear wheels turn on the mainshaft, driven by the layshaft but not driving anything themselves. When one of the three, four or five gears is required, it is locked to the mainshaft, rather than being slid along it as in the sliding-mesh gearbox or 'crash-box', and thus drive from layshaft to mainshaft is obtained. The constant-mesh

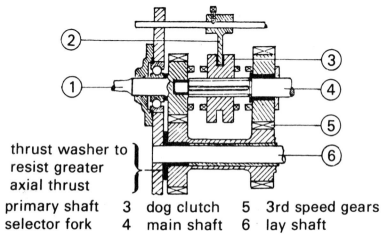

thrust washer to
resist greater
axial thrust

1 primary shaft	3 dog clutch	5 3rd speed gears
2 selector fork	4 main shaft	6 lay shaft

Fig. 1.8. In the constant-mesh gearbox the mainshaft gear wheels are free to rotate on the mainshaft but are locked to it by the dog clutch projections

Fig. 1.9. Gear wheels with a helical tooth form are in permanent mesh

gearbox has two obvious advantages over the sliding-mesh type:

1. The gear teeth do not have to be cut straight as they are permanently meshed and there is no requirement for them to slide together.
2. Any damage caused to the teeth of the sliding-mesh-type gear wheels due to poor driver-synchronization is confined to the locking mechanism on the side of each constant-mesh mainshaft gear wheel rather than to the gear wheel teeth themselves.

Straight-cut gears are very noisy in use, causing the whining noise that you often hear old tractors or racing cars making. Incidentally, the Mini power unit (which can be found in Allegros and Metros also) has a straight-cut first gear, for reasons which we will not go into at this stage, so listen to the next one that pulls away within your earshot and you will appreciate the distinctive difference in sound between first and all other gears.

By cutting the tooth form of a gearbox gear wheel *helically* so that each tooth describes a gently curved ridge as in Fig. 1.9, and has a rounded profile, the force transmitted from the tooth of one gear wheel to the tooth of another is applied progressively in a rolling action, thereby generating considerably less noise. The meshing of helical teeth, though, has the associated complication of generating *thrust*—the sideways pushing of the gear wheels due to some of the force transmitted from one tooth to another being in a direction in line with the gearbox shafts.

This sideways force acting on the gear wheels and ultimately on the shafts has to be resisted by *thrust washers*, which are bearings so designed as to allow the rotating parts to turn while pushing against them, though they must create the minimum amount of friction or braking action on those parts in so doing. Bearings are dealt with in greater detail in chapter 4.

Returning to the operation of the constant-mesh-type gearbox, the mainshaft gear wheels are individually locked to the shaft by means of dog clutches, one half of which is permanently splined to the shaft and positioned next to the gear wheel (one is located between each pair of gear wheels on a four-speed gearbox). The moveable half of the dog clutch is a rotating hub with a central peripheral groove (Fig. 1.8) in which the selector fork runs, in turn indirectly connected to the gear lever inside the car. Each gear wheel has large castellations on its side which form the other half of the dog clutches. When the hub is moved along the mainshaft towards a gear wheel by the selector mechanism, the projections of both gear wheel and sleeve engage and the gear wheel is thereby locked to the shaft. But of course double-declutching is still required as the dog teeth will otherwise clash, though gear wheel damage is avoided.

Constant load synchromesh

In all modern roadgoing cars fitted with manual transmission, *synchromesh* is used to match gear speeds automatically for the driver. In the synchromesh gearbox the two dog clutches of the simple constant-mesh box which sit between first/second and third/fourth gear wheels respectively are replaced with *synchronizers*. The synchronizer of the simple *constant load* system (the first, and now obsolete, type of synchromesh) comprises two elements: the central hub which is splined to the mainshaft and is free to move along it to a certain extent in either direction, and the outer sleeve which is splined to the hub and is also free to slide one way or another along it (Fig. 1.10). The synchronizer sleeve has a peripheral groove in which the selector fork is located, just as in the simple constant-mesh gearbox. A conical projection extends from the side of each mainshaft gear wheel towards the synchronizer, which component has a corresponding conical recess on each side of the hub; these two conical members together form a *cone clutch*. Each gear wheel carries a ring of small dog teeth at its side, positioned at the base (gear-wheel side) of the cone (2, Fig. 1.10), and these are machined to match the splines on the underside of the synchronizer sleeve to achieve a locking mechanism between gear wheel and synchronizer.

When the gear lever is moved to select a gear, the rotating synchronizer is slid along its hub towards the relevant gear wheel and initial contact between the two is

Fig. 1.10. Constant load synchromesh

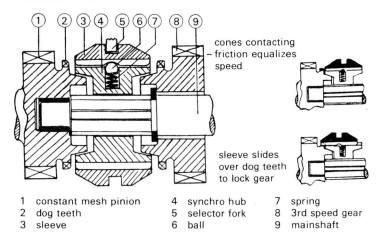

cones contacting – friction equalizes speed

sleeve slides over dog teeth to lock gear

1	constant mesh pinion	4	synchro hub	7	spring
2	dog teeth	5	selector fork	8	3rd speed gear
3	sleeve	6	ball	9	mainshaft

via the cone clutch. This progressively transmits torque from the synchronizer hub to the gear wheel as its male and female components are pushed together, bringing them to the same speed. A series of spring-loaded balls are carried in radial holes in the synchronizer hub (6, Fig. 1.10) and these push outwards into a central groove on the underside of the sleeve. These sprung balls ensure that when the sleeve is pushed by the selector fork, it will carry the hub with it. When the cone clutch is fully engaged, however— and so gear wheel and hub are both turning at a synchronized speed—and the hub can go no further, final movement of the gear lever will overcome the pressure exerted on the sleeve by the sprung balls and the sleeve will then slide towards the gear wheel independently of the hub, to effect dog-tooth engagement and thus a locked drive. The edges of the splines and the dog teeth are bevelled in order to ensure that engagement will be achieved every time. The need for double-declutching is eliminated, as simple movement of the gear lever is all that the driver need concern himself with to achieve a synchronized change of gear.

The system has one obvious weakness though, in that unless the gearchange is made carefully, and reasonably slowly, the synchromesh will not have time to work and the dog teeth will clash before gear wheel and mainshaft are running at the same speed. The time which it takes for the two speeds to be equalized is determined by the frictional force existing at the two faces of the cone clutch, and this force is a function of the angle of the cone clutch, the coefficient of friction available at the clutch, the strength of the synchronizer detent springs and the depth and angle of the detent groove in the underside of the sleeves. If, for any reason, one or more of these factors is impaired, then it will be all too easy to 'beat the synchro' and achieve a grating gearchange. This will damage the dog teeth and maybe even fail to engage the gear.

Yet another factor which can adversely affect the efficiency of the synchromesh is the thickness of the gearbox oil which, generally speaking, needs to be thick to withstand the high pressures of gear tooth contact. Unfortunately, thick or *viscous* oil is not easily squeezed away by the conical clutch faces of the synchromesh and so hinders synchronization. To alleviate the problem, one of the cone faces has rows of fine grooves machined around its surface so that the oil can be cut into and more readily dispersed (Fig. 1.12).

Modern proportional load synchromesh

Today's synchromesh gearboxes are best technically described as *proportional load* synchromesh to differentiate them from this early *constant load* type. The proportional load synchro is so called because it comprises additional features to ensure that the pressure with which the cone clutch is engaged is proportional to the gearchange force, thus preventing overriding of the synchromesh action due to hasty operation of the lever.

In a typical proportional load synchromesh, a ring is interposed between gear wheel cone and synchronizer hub (Fig. 1.11) and the hub is prevented from any sideways movement, unlike in the earlier type. This ring, known as the *baulk ring* (*baulk*, in this context meaning *to refuse* or *hinder*) forms the female component of the cone clutch (previously machined into the synchronizer hub) and it is free to move sideways slightly when the gear is not engaged. It also carries the fine oil-cutting grooves on its conical inside surface (Fig. 1.12). As can be seen in Fig. 1.11, the baulk ring has a set of bevelled dog teeth at its outer edge, which perfectly match those to be found on the

Fig. 1.11. Modern proportional load synchromesh. This common type features a baulk ring

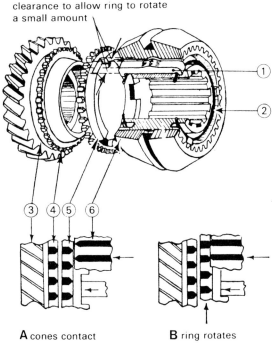

clearance to allow ring to rotate
a small amount

A cones contact   B ring rotates

1 shifting plate	4 gear dog teeth
2 circlip spring	5 baulking cone and ring
3 gear	6 sleeve

Fig. 1.12. Fine grooves on inside taper of baulk ring (the female cone of the cone clutch) serve to disperse gearbox oil; oil is then fed out of the cone clutch via axial channels

gear wheel and on the underside of the synchro sleeve. It also has three cut-outs in the edge which faces the synchronizer and these line up with three *blocker bars* (also sometimes known as shifting plates, keys or slippers) located in longitudinal recesses between synchro hub and synchro sleeve, sprung upwards into the sleeve either by coil springs as in Fig. 1.10, or sprung circlips (Fig. 1.11).

When the gear lever is moved to select a gear, the fork in the synchronizer sleeve pushes the sleeve, blocker bars and baulk ring into light 'brushing' contact with the gear wheel cone and, as the three cut-outs in the ring are slightly wider than the protruding blocker bars, this friction is sufficient to allow the ring to be dragged around (due to the difference in speed between synchronizer and gear wheel) as far as the cut-outs will allow, before being stopped by the bars.

The cut-outs are wider than the blocker bars only by an amount which equates to half a dog-tooth pitch and this rotational loading will put the baulk ring teeth out of position with the synchro sleeve teeth so that instead of meshing they butt up against each other (B, Fig. 1.11). Further pressure on the gear lever moves the sleeve towards the gear wheel dog teeth, but while the two are turning at different speeds the baulk ring teeth are still so aligned as to refuse mesh with the sleeve splines. As more pressure is exerted on the gear lever, the baulk ring and gear wheel cone are forced together harder and the speeds of the two progressively synchronize. As soon as they are both turning at the same speed there is no longer a unidirectional loading on the baulk ring and so final lever movement can allow the sleeve teeth to bevel the baulk ring teeth into line, thereby allowing the sleeve to slide over the ring and the gear wheel dog teeth.

Some examples of synchromesh

Although all proportional load synchromesh devices do exactly the same job, they do not all do it in the same way, nor do they all use the same components. Some types (Peugeot synchromesh, for instance) do not even use a separate baulk ring but incorporate the baulking function into the synchronizer unit in one neat package (Fig. 1.13). Leyland cars using the trusty front-wheel-drive 'gears-in-sump' transmission have baulk rings, although these have no dog-tooth set around them and there are no blocker bars to be found in the system (Fig. 1.14).

Again, other variations of the theme exist but the Ford, Peugeot and Leyland 'gears-in-sump' types are probably three excellent examples of how a small mechanism with the common function of synchronizing gears can be executed in quite radically different ways. With the operation of these three types of synchronizer understood, you should be able to comprehend the construction of any other type that you are presented with, however different it is.

The type already described and illustrated is that used in certain General Motors cars and similar to the Ford type, which also uses sprung circlips in the synchronizer hub

Fig. 1.13. A Peugeot synchronizer incorporates the function of the baulk ring in one unit with the hub and selector sleeve

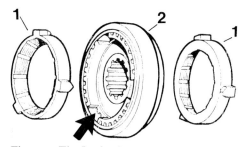

Fig. 1.14. The Leyland synchromesh assembly: (1) baulk ring; (2) synchronizer

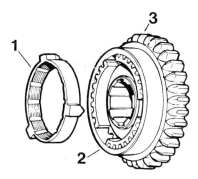

Fig. 1.15. A Leyland first/second-gear synchronizer (2) with straight-cut peripheral teeth; this serves as the mainshaft first and reverse gear wheels (3)—baulk ring labelled '1'

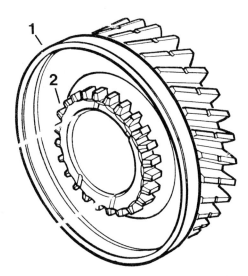

Fig. 1.16. A Peugeot gear wheel. The large disc at its side is the female part of the synchronizer cone clutch (1), while the small straight-cut teeth on the inside are the dog teeth (2) which hold the gear in engagement

(rather than coil springs with detent balls) and blocker bars.

As an aside, and to avoid any possible confusion at this stage, you may possibly have noticed that some synchronizer sleeves appear to have a peripheral set of straight-cut gear teeth (Fig. 1.15); this is a commonly used, space-saving means of providing a reverse gear without having to extend the mainshaft to accommodate an extra gear wheel. A reverse gear *idler*, identical in function to that described in our initial section on sliding-mesh gearboxes, is positioned at a point near the sleeve and slid into mesh with it and a corresponding layshaft gear, to provide a suitable ratio for reversing and to reverse the direction of mainshaft rotation. Straight-cut gear teeth can be employed for reverse gear as the extra noise generated is not a problem for the length of time the car is likely to be reversing.

Some cars, notably those that use the Leyland 'gears-in-sump' unit and also the original Datsun Cherry, have a dual-function straight-cut gear on one of the synchronizers, that also serves as a sliding-mesh first gear for the purposes if space- and cost-saving. The extra noise is considered insignificant for the same reason it is with reverse gear. This type is the exception though, rather than the rule.

Returning to the subject of synchromesh devices though, the Peugeot item shown in Fig. 1.13 (which is similar to the type employed by Buick) is a fascinating device in that it comprises only two basic separate parts: the splined hub, which is fixed to the mainshaft, and the 'sleeve' which also serves as the male part of the cone clutch rather than the more usual female. The gear wheels are similarly unusual (Fig. 1.16) in that the female cone is in the form of a large-diameter pressed-steel dish shrunk to the side of the gear wheel and a small-diameter ring of dog teeth resides within it. The selector fork locates in the central groove of the synchronizer and sideways movement of the fork pushes the whole sleeve/cone assembly into light contact with the cone of the gear wheel, against internal, upward spring pressure from a circular spring ring. This causes drag to occur on the synchronizer cone.

The three hardened-steel pins which connect the two

sides of the synchronizer together (arrowed, Fig. 1.17) are sharply waisted in the middle at the point where they pass through holes in the splined centre portion of the sleeve. As they are of smaller diameter than the holes they pass through, the centre (splined) portion of the assembly and the two outer clutch surfaces can be rotated through a couple of millimetres independently of each other (just as the loose fit of the blocker bar ends in the previously mentioned baulk ring cut-outs allowed a small amount of rotation of the rings). With the clutch surfaces loaded in one direction then, the centre splined section of the synchronizer cannot be pushed further towards the gear wheel as it is prevented from doing so by the step in the through-pins. But any further pressure on the lever will produce greater friction between gear wheel and synchronizer clutch faces and thus their speeds will progressively be equalized at a rate proportional to the amount of force being exerted at the gear lever. Once both are running at the same speed the pins will no longer be loaded against one extreme of the holes in the centre section and final lever movement will bevel the waisted pins to centre themselves, thus allowing full engagement of the internal synchronizer splines and the pinion dog teeth.

Fig. 1.17. The hardened steel pins connecting together the two sides of the Peugeot synchronizer are waisted in the middle to allow the two male cones to 'jiggle' in the elongated holes of the hub/selector sleeve; this allows the pins to be loaded to one side of the holes in order to prevent gear engagement when drag is occurring at the clutch surfaces

The Leyland 'gears-in-sump' type (Mini) design of synchromesh employs a conventional gear pinion which has a projecting cone at its side as the male component of the cone clutch, and a ring of dog teeth at the base of this cone. The teeth correspond to splines on the underside of the synchronizer sleeve and the splined synchronizer hub is fixed to the mainshaft. It differs from the GM/Ford type in not having dog teeth on the baulk ring but rather three externally projecting radial lugs (Fig. 1.14) which correspond with recesses in the synchro hub (arrowed, Fig. 1.14). The lugs are narrower than these recesses and so the ring is free to 'jiggle' rotationally.

Over the hub and baulk ring sits the splined sleeve (just as in the previous designs) and the underside of the sleeve has three channels to accommodate the lugs. These channels are not wider than the lugs, however, except at their ends, where they open out into a 'V' shape, the ramps of which are at 45 degrees and correspond with the pointed

Fig. 1.18. The Peugeot-type
synchronizer and gear wheel
held in alignment

tapers of the baulk ring lugs. As axial movement of the synchronizer sleeve pushes the baulk ring into contact with the gear pinion cone, the difference in speed between pinion and synchronizer, and the light friction of the cone clutch, loads the baulk ring in one direction so that its lugs butt up against one side of the 'V' ramp. While the lugs are held like this against the ramps, the synchronizer sleeve cannot travel any further axially, as the lugs will not engage with the channels in the underside of the sleeve.

However, as friction between the cone clutch faces increases (due to continual pressure on the gear lever), the speed difference between pinion and synchronizer decreases until the speeds are matched, at which point the baulk ring is no longer loaded in any direction and its lugs bevel themselves into the channels by means of their taper shape.

Thus further travel of the synchronizer sleeve engages the pinion dog teeth with the splines on the underside of the sleeve, effecting total gear engagement.

Chapter 2 | Transmission layouts

Many different transmissions have been used during the development of the car into its relatively refined present-day form. Originally belts were a common method of power transmission, giving way to chains, which survived in the gearbox and final drive of the Frazer-Nash right up to 1939. Chains are still used as a primary-drive transfer method in some Saabs and American cars, particularly automatics, but have largely given way to shafts and gears in manual cars.

Clutches have evolved from simply ways of tightening the transmission belts to increase friction and engage drive through cone, drum, and multi-plate clutches of both wet (i.e. oil immersed) and dry varieties, to today's almost universal single-plate diaphragm spring clutch.

Ratio selection was absent in early cars, but the advantages were soon discovered and many different methods of achieving it devised. The first practical and robust method was the sliding-mesh gearbox, though anyone used to today's cars would probably disagree. Next in the process of refinement came the constant-mesh dog-clutch gearbox and finally the full synchromesh gearbox.

Though great advances have been made in the components of the car transmission, equally great changes have occurred in the physical layout of the components within the chassis. The possible physical layouts do, of course, depend on the drive medium used, but with the adoption of gear and shaft drives has come a lot of design freedom. Recently pressures of fuel economy and space efficiency have forced greater uniformity in design, as shown by the vast number of small transverse-engine front-wheel-drive cars now produced. This tendency towards uniformity of layout has, however, occurred principally in the last ten years and quite diverse layouts were used during the period of car manufacture covered by this manual.

The object of this chapter is to describe some of the more popular ones so that the reader can appreciate the important differences. The cars used as examples have been chosen to include the majority of different layouts used.

1) Rear-wheel-drive, overdrive and live axle: Jaguar Mk 2

Transmission layouts of the type used by Jaguar on the Mk 2 (Fig. 2.1) were once the most common arrangement in use on cars of all sizes. Though the Jaguar Mk 2 had by the standards of the day a relatively refined rear suspension system, consisting of cantilever leaf springs, torque arms

Fig. 2.1. Jaguar Mk 2 transmission layout of the Hotchkiss type: 1 rear road spring; 2 front mounting pad; 3 front mounting plate; 4 centre clamping plate; 5 torque arm; 6 panhard rod; 7 panhard rod (adjusting piece); 8 panhard rod (locknut); 9 panhard rod (rubber buffer); 10 panhard rod (distance tube); 11 panhard rod (outer washer); 12 panhard rod (inner washer); 13 hydraulic damper; 14 hydraulic damper (rubber buffer); 15 hydraulic damper (inner washer); 16 hydraulic damper (outer washer); 17 hydraulic damper (securing nut); 18 hydraulic damper (locknut)

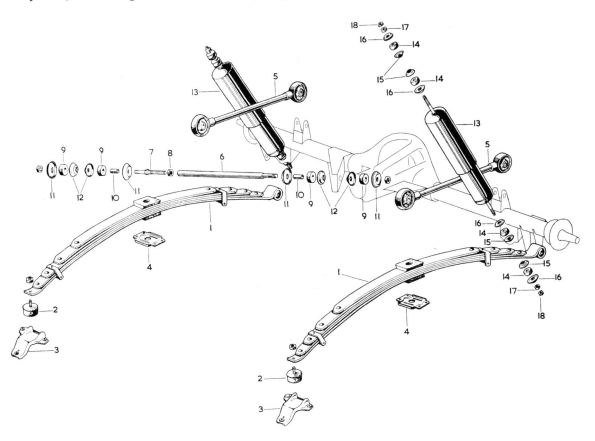

and a panhard rod, it retained the hypoid live axle and three-synchro gearbox typical of other cars at the time.

The Mk 2 was also available with a Laycock de Normanville overdrive unit, which was a very common fitment to many larger cars, as the five-speed gearbox was uncommon.

This 'Hotchkiss' layout continued in use in many cars right up until the end of the 1970s, when independent rear suspension became widely used.

The Mk 2 had a single-dry-plate clutch clamped by a coil spring clutch cover in early models, later changed to a diaphragm spring cover. A four-speed gearbox was used on all models, the earlier version (Fig. 2.2) having no synchromesh on first gear and non-baulk ring synchromesh with no blocking mechanism, while the later version had baulk ring synchromesh on all forward gears. The gearboxes had direct-drive fourth gears and indirect intermediates (chapter 4).

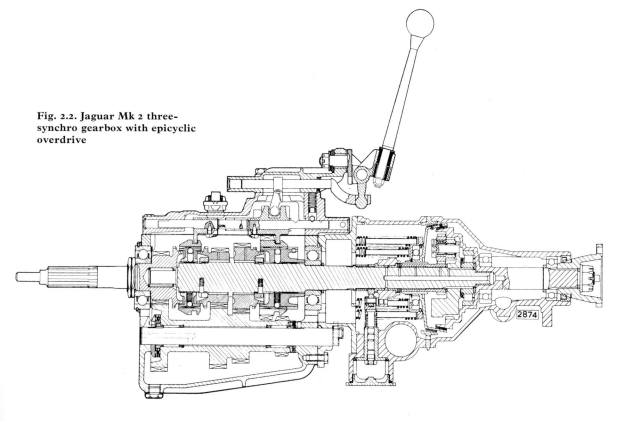

Fig. 2.2. Jaguar Mk 2 three-synchro gearbox with epicyclic overdrive

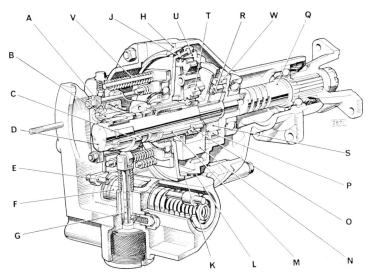

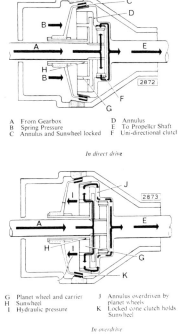

A From Gearbox   D Annulus
B Spring Pressure   E To Propeller Shaft
C Annulus and Sunwheel locked F Uni-directional clutch

In direct drive

G Planet wheel and carrier   J Annulus overdriven by
H Sunwheel   planet wheels
I Hydraulic pressure   K Locked cone clutch holds
                                   Sunwheel

In overdrive

Fig. 2.3. Laycock de Normanville overdrive showing planetary gearing and conical friction clutch arrangement

The overdrive unit, where fitted, replaced the gearbox tailshaft housing and consisted of a single planetary gearset engaged by an oil hydraulic circuit and controlled by a solenoid valve (Fig. 2.3). The overdrive input shaft drives the planet gear carrier and the output is taken from the annulus. The sun gear is clamped by the hydraulically operated cone clutch either to the output shaft, producing direct drive, or to the overdrive casing, producing a step-up ratio of 0.778:1. The clutch hydraulic circuit is powered by an oil pump in the overdrive unit, which shares the same oil as the gearbox and, where a pressure-lubricated gearbox is fitted, also supplies oil to the gearbox. Overdrive can only be engaged when fourth gear is selected, as the unit cannot carry the greater torque produced in lower gears, and engagement is prevented by an electrical interlock (Fig. 2.4). Overdrive units are usually classed with automatic transmissions as non-serviceable items and, unless a fault is in the overdrive electrical circuit, an exchange unit should be purchased. Clogging of the often overlooked oil filter in the overdrive unit can cause slippage or complete failure of engagement so this should always be checked before assuming damage to the unit.

The propshaft is one-piece with Hooke's joints at either end and carries drive to the hypoid bevel differential

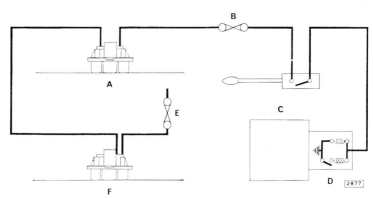

A Top gear switch
B Fuse (Overdrive in-line)
C Manual switch
D Solenoid
E Fuse (Ignition auxiliary)
F Reverse lamp switch

Fig. 2.4. Overdrive electrical actuation on Jaguar gearbox; note the lockout switches preventing overdrive selection in the lower gears and reverse

mounted in the live axle casing. The differential runs in taper roller bearings in bearing caps accessible through the rear cover and also supports the inner ends of the solid unjointed halfshafts. Mesh adjustment is by shims behind the differential and pinion bearings.

Some Mk 2s were fitted with a Thornton 'Powr-lok' limited slip differential (chapter 5), which was a direct replacement for the normal units.

2) Rear-wheel-drive, independent suspension: Sierra

The transmission layout used in the Ford Sierra (Fig. 2.5) is typical of the type used in more modern rear-wheel-drive cars with independent suspension. Layouts of this type have only recently been used in the medium saloon class of cars, to which the Sierra belongs, as manufacturers dropped live rear axle suspensions to improve ride and handling.

The layout is less space efficient than the transverse, front-wheel-drive layout adopted by many of the Sierra's competitors, e.g. the Vauxhall Cavalier and Austin Montego, but has an advantage where relatively powerful engines are used. Torque steer is absent and a more neutral and consistent handling balance can be obtained with good suspension design.

The only alternative to this layout in higher power cars to offer similar or better handling is a four-wheel-drive one, which is more expensive and complicated to manufacture, and hence less popular.

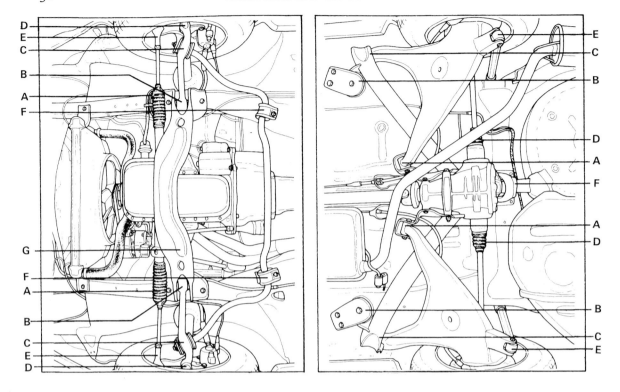

Fig. 2.5. Sierra transmission layout—a modern rear-wheel-drive, independent suspension layout

The engine is mounted inline at the front of the car and drives through a clutch and gearbox mounted on the back of the engine to form a single power unit. Again a single-dry-plate clutch is used, in this case with cable actuation. A splined gearbox input shaft passes into the front of the very conventional gearbox. The gearbox has a 1:1 ratio direct-drive fourth gear, while the lower gears are all indirect. Some models are fitted with a five-speed gearbox, which has an extra indirect overdrive ratio gearset mounted in the tailshaft housing, to the rear of the back bearing web (Fig. 2.6). Ratio selection is by a single selector shaft above the mainshaft, running forward from the tailshaft-mounted gear lever to the individual selector forks.

The propshaft has three joints. The forward one at the gearbox output may be of the Hooke's or rubber doughnut type, while the joints at the propshaft centre mounting and final drive input are always Hooke's joints.

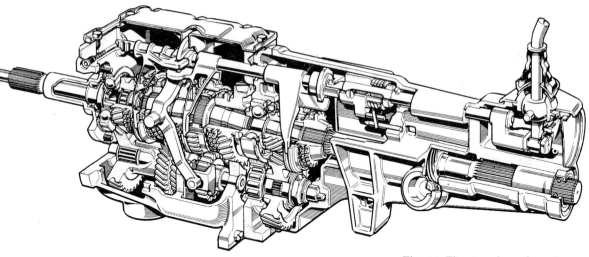

Fig. 2.6. Five-speed gearbox of the Sierra; note the simple single selector shaft and the fifth-gear wheels housed in the tail casing

The final drive is contained in a light alloy casing mounted on the rear suspension cross tube. A helical bevel non-hypoid gear type (chapter 5) is used for the final drive pinion and crown wheel, as there is less constraint on the level of entry of the propeller shaft with independent suspension and non-hypoid gears are less prone to wear. The bevel gear differential is entirely conventional and is supported by bearings on both sides of the casing, which are adjustable by means of threaded flanges to set the gear mesh and preload the bearings.

Solid driveshafts with tripodal joints at both ends are used as the angular movement of the shafts is relatively small.

3) Rear-wheel-drive, rear inline engine: Beetle

The Volkswagen Beetle (Fig. 2.7) is an example of a rear engine and transaxle layout. The same arrangement was used on Variants and similar ones on the Renault Dauphine and rear-engined Porsches. The transmission is termed a 'transaxle' as both the gearbox (transmission) and final drive (axle) are housed within the same compact casing.

Fig. 2.7. VW Beetle transmission layout—an inline rear engine layout with dubious handling characteristics

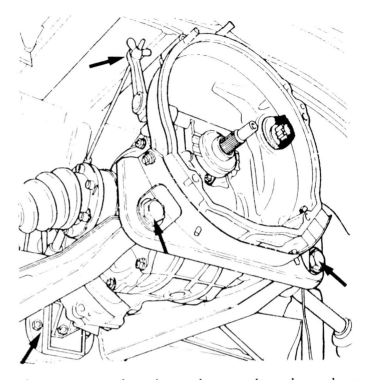

A rear-mounted engine and transaxle make a cheap, compact power unit, as intended by Ferdinand Porsche for his 'people's car', but, especially when used with a swing axle rear suspension system like the Beetle's, also give a 'tail-happy' handling balance. This was not particularly important as the early Beetles were massively underpowered, but became a problem as the engine power was increased.

Rear transaxles are also used in mid-engined cars with inline engines, such as the Ford GT40, which display a much better handling manner.

Beetles employ a single-dry-plate clutch mounted in the transaxle casing just behind the rear axle line (in front of the engine). Clutch actuation is by cable and drive is taken over the differential to the gearbox by an extension of the gearbox input shaft. The gearbox is a four-speed all-indirect four-synchromesh type on later cars and has the unusual feature that the two synchronizer hubs are mounted on different shafts. The input shaft carries the

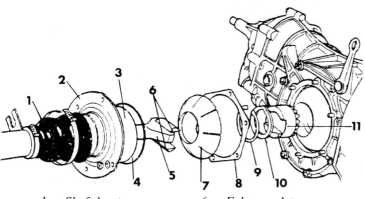

Fig. 2.8. VW Beetle swing axle—the axle halfshafts pivot about these part-spherical covers, either side of the differential

1.	Shaft boot	6.	Fulcrum plates
2.	Retaining ring	7.	Hemispherical packing piece
3.	Axle casing domed end	8.	Gasket shim
4.	'O' ring seal	9.	Circlip
5.	Axle shaft spade end	10.	Thrust ring
		11.	Side gear

first- and second-gear fixed gears at the rear and the third- and fourth-gear synchronizer and free gears at the front. The shaft below it in the casing, which also carries the final drive pinion, carries the first- and second-gear synchronizer and free gears and the third- and fourth-speed fixed gears.

The final drive is a helical bevel gear pair and the differential of the bevel gear type with larger than normal output gears to accommodate the ends of the swing axle shafts. The swing axle suspension, fitted to the Beetle until the mid-1970s, uses the transaxle to locate the inner ends of the axles so the transaxle is strengthened to accept side loads on the differential, which is mounted in very large bearings in the side cover plates (Fig. 2.8).

The axle shaft outer casings are connected to the side cover plates by part-spherical bearing surfaces, while the axle shafts themselves have unusual, but simple and effective, two-piece non-constant velocity joints within the differential output gears (Fig. 2.9).

The Beetle gearbox is a rugged design and has been used in many other custom-made vehicles with a variety of different engines. It was also the basis for the famous Hewland racing gearbox.

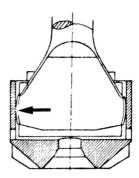

Fig. 2.9. Swing-axle joints of the VW Beetle. These simple non-constant velocity joints transmit the drive to the halfshafts

4) Rear-wheel-drive, front engine, rear gearbox: Alfetta

Alfa Romeo are one of the few European car makers, besides Porsche and Volvo, to produce cars with this particular transmission layout (Fig. 2.10). The same layout is also used in other cars in their range, the Giulietta and GTV, principally because of the benefit to handling of the more even front:rear weight distribution it allows. Sporty handling seems to be one of the main considerations of the Alfa Romeo buyer and, due to this, Alfa Romeo can afford the increased complication and expense of a more exotic transmission layout and the often criticized baulky gearchange quality. This layout is not used by other higher volume car makers because of these same disadvantages.

Other disadvantages on the Alfetta are the difficulty of changing the clutch plate and restricted access to the rear brake pads.

Fig. 2.10. The Alfetta transmission layout gives a very good weight distribution but poor access

1 - De Dion axle
2 - Transverse link
3 - Anti-roll bar
4 - Bump rubber
5 - Spring
6 - Shock-absorber

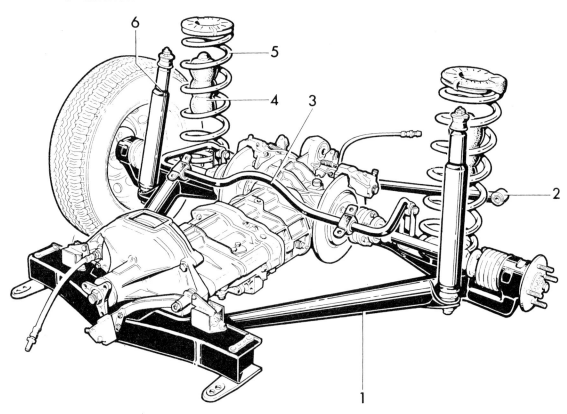

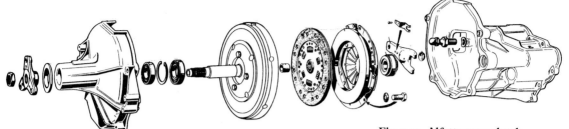

Fig. 2.11. Alfetta rear clutch 'flywheel'—this component and arrangement is unique to rear gearbox cars and can give propshaft vibration problems

The inline engine of the Alfetta is fitted with a smaller than usual flywheel enclosed in an alloy cover, which also serves as the rear engine mounting bracket. The propshaft is connected directly to the flywheel by a flexible doughnut-type joint and passes through the alloy cover to the rear transaxle. The propshaft has a floor-pan-mounted centre bearing and two more doughnut joints at the centre bearing and at the input to the transaxle. The propshaft is of the usual tubular steel construction but, because a significant part of the effective flywheel inertia comes from the rear-mounted clutch 'flywheel' (Fig. 2.11), it is carefully constructed and balanced to prevent the torsional vibrations which can occur with such a layout.

The clutch is housed behind the front transaxle cover plate and consists of a heavy hub, on which a normal single-dry-plate clutch cover is mounted. The clutch is hydraulically actuated and the whole clutch assembly is supported on the input shaft bearings in the front cover, which also take the thrust load from the clutch release bearings.

A splined shaft carries the drive to an all-indirect two-shaft five-speed gearbox (Fig. 2.12). The input shaft carries the five fixed gears, while the output shaft, below it in the casing, carries the five free gears and Porsche ring synchronizer hubs (chapter 4). The final drive is of a non-hypoid helical bevel type and sits in the rear section of the transaxle casing, sharing oil with the gearbox. Adjustment of the final drive mesh is by a distance piece at the opposite end of the output shaft and by shims behind the differential bearings in the differential housing and side access cover.

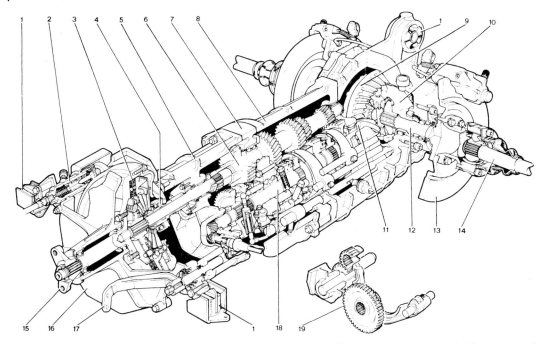

Fig. 2.12. The Alfetta gearbox is similar to an inline front-wheel-drive transaxle

Flanges on each differential output shaft carry the inboard-mounted brake discs and the Birfield-type constant velocity joints of the driveshafts.

5) Front-wheel-drive, transverse, gearbox-in-sump: Mini

The Mini, first entering production in 1958, set a pattern for small car transmission layouts (Fig. 2.13). The use of a transverse engine and front-wheel drive was the only way to get the efficiency of space utilization required in a small four-seater car and this has been copied by many manufacturers since. Inline engine layouts only survive in the larger luxury front-wheel-drive cars, such as Audis and Saabs, with Renault being perhaps the last volume manufacturer to abandon this layout in the small car sector.

Front-wheel drive was not a new idea when the Mini was designed, but the ingenious use of a transverse engine above the gearbox must be credited to Sir Alec Issigonis. The arrangement was not initially without problems. During development the engine had to be turned through

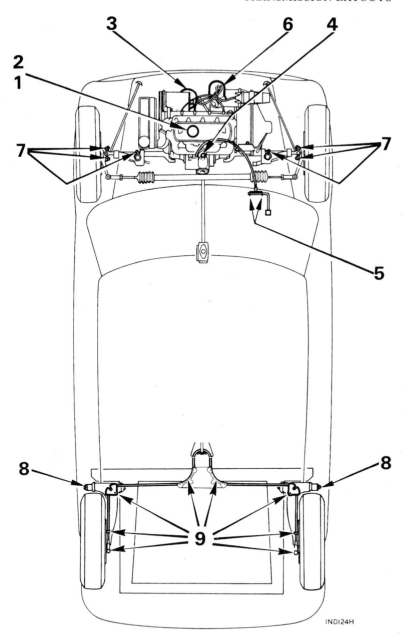

Fig. 2.13. The 'gearbox-in-sump' transverse layout of the Mini set the pattern that was later followed by many small cars

INDI24H

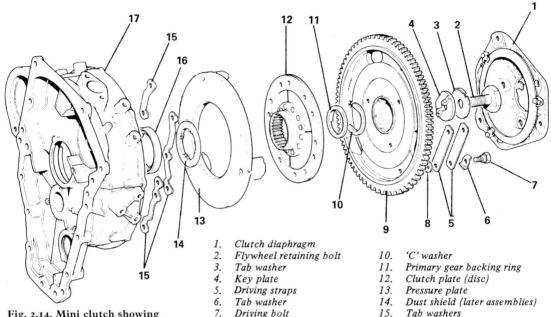

Fig. 2.14. Mini clutch showing the unusual inverted flywheel/pressure plate arrangement

1. Clutch diaphragm
2. Flywheel retaining bolt
3. Tab washer
4. Key plate
5. Driving straps
6. Tab washer
7. Driving bolt
8. Washer
9. Flywheel
10. 'C' washer
11. Primary gear backing ring
12. Clutch plate (disc)
13. Pressure plate
14. Dust shield (later assemblies)
15. Tab washers
16. Flywheel housing oil seal
17. Flywheel housing

180 degrees from its original orientation due to persistent carburettor icing. This change necessitated the introduction of an idler gear between engine and gearbox, which was at the time considered easier than changing the direction of rotation of the engine, but has since proved to be one of the most troublesome parts in the Mini transmission.

The Mini clutch (Fig. 2.14) is unusual in that the driven plate is behind the flywheel and is clamped by a pressure plate with lugs that pass through the flywheel to the clutch cover. At first a coil spring clutch was used but this was later changed to a diaphragm spring type. Drive is passed from the clutch-driven plate to a primary drive gear, which is free to rotate on the engine crankshaft. This engages with an idler gear mounted below it in the transfer gear casing, which meshes with the gearbox input shaft gear.

The Mini gearbox (Fig. 2.15), though transversely mounted, is very similar to previous Austin designs with a direct top gear and indirect intermediates. Power enters the gearbox at the clutch end of the mainshaft and leaves it at the opposite end of the mainshaft, which passes through a support bearing to the final drive pinion. The final drive is of a spur gear type, as the final drive pinion axis is parallel to the differential axis. Driveshafts with flexible rubber inner joints connect to the hubs with Rzeppa constant velocity joints at the hub end. An equal and opposite torque to that driving the wheels acts on the whole power unit and puts a high load on the engine mountings in this arrangement.

The Mini gearbox shares its lubricant with the engine, which is good as its temperature is thus kept more constant, but can be the cause of gearbox damage if the oil becomes contaminated by the engine. Gearbox problems are fairly frequent in Minis and other cars sharing the same transmission, with noisy idler gears and loss of synchromesh being the most common.

Fig. 2.15. This four-speed, four-synchro gearbox of the Mini drew much from earlier Austin rear-wheel-drive gearbox experience

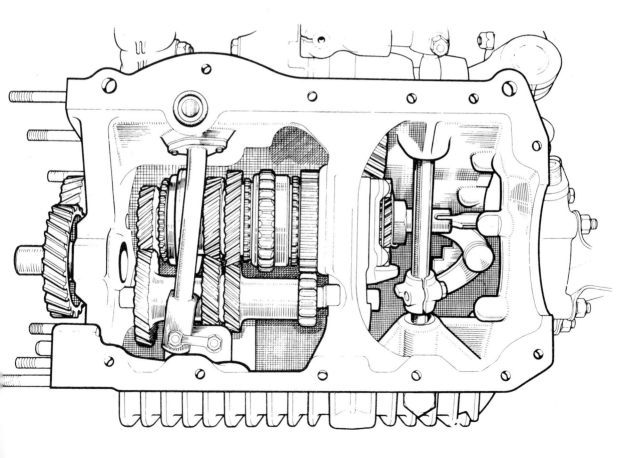

6) Front-wheel-drive, inline engine: Renault 5

The Renault 5 had similar success in France to that enjoyed by the Mini in England, and catered for the same part of the market. The transmission was a smaller step from Renault's previous rear-engine practice than the Mini's was from Austin's rear-wheel-drive designs. For this reason Renault made fewer mistakes than Austin and came up with a reliable long-lasting transmission for their first front-wheel-drive mini-car.

The engines in the Renault 5 range are all mounted inline and drive the wheels through the unique Renault arrangement of clutch and gearbox in front of the engine (Fig. 2.16). This arrangement has the disadvantage of making engine access difficult and detracts from passenger space within the car, where there is a large engine intrusion between the foot wells. Renault have changed the layout in their new 5s and have adopted the standard 'Eurobox' transverse engine and gearbox.

Fig. 2.16. The Renault 5 transmission layout is less space-efficient than the Mini's and has now been superseded

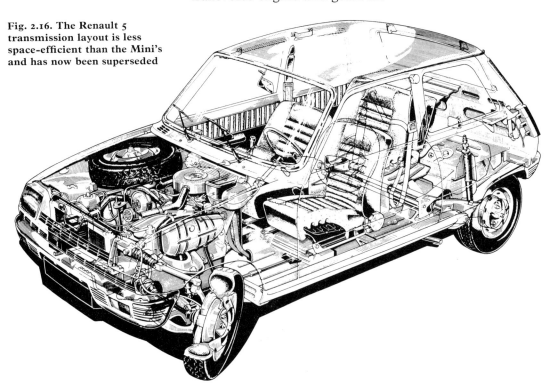

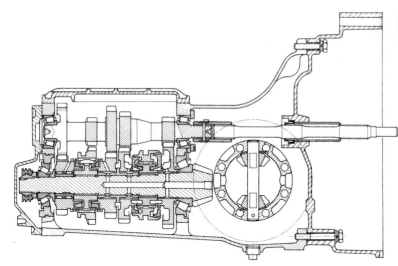

The clutch on the Renault 5 is of conventional single-dry-plate diaphragm spring type and transmits drive through a splined gearbox input shaft like that employed on front-engine rear-wheel-drive cars. The difference is that it passes over the final drive to the all-indirect gearbox, both of which are contained in the same cast housing. Several models of gearbox have been fitted to the Renault 5, but all have been similar in basic design, as indeed are the gearboxes fitted to all Renault inline engine cars. The upper shaft in the gearbox (Fig. 2.17) looks like the layshaft in a rear-wheel-drive gearbox, but does not perform the same function, as it transmits the drive to the mainshaft in all gears and never idles. The mainshaft sits below this and carries the synchronizer hubs and gears for four or five ratios. If five ratios are fitted then the fifth gear and synchronizer are housed in an extended end casing in front of the end-bearing support web (Fig. 2.18).

The bevel gear final drive is not a hypoid type (chapter 5), as common in live rear axles, but a plain bevel, and is supported at the level of the mainshaft by bearings in both sides of the gearbox casing. Final drive alignment is by means of these bearings, which are positioned laterally in the casing by large lockable threaded collars (Fig. 2.19).

Driveshafts with tripodal joints, the inner ones being of the plunging variety, drive the front wheels.

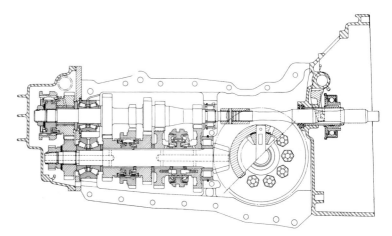

Fig. 2.18. The Renault 5 fifth-gear arrangement. As in many gearboxes, the fifth-gear components are an addition to the four-speed gearbox

The position of the gearbox in front of the engine made for a complicated gearchange linkage and early 5s were fitted with a dash-mounted umbrella change with the linkage passing over the top of the engine. This simple and quick linkage was changed for a rubbery floor-mounted one on later models.

7) Front-wheel-drive, transverse, end-mounted gearbox: Astra

This arrangement used by Vauxhall on the Astra (Fig. 2.20) and also by Ford, Fiat, Renault and Peugeot on small and medium-sized volume production cars is the most modern and space efficient layout described in this section. A gearbox mounted on the end of the engine has advantages over the Mini's layout in allowing a lower bonnet line and centre of gravity and making the clutch and gearbox more accessible. The main disadvantages of the layout are that engines with more than four cylinders are not easily accommodated, due to the restricted width, and that a front-wheel-drive layout is not in any case desirable with engines above about 150 hp, as there are traction problems. On smaller cars with this layout the more usual (and cheaper) unequal-length driveshafts (chapter 6) can also produce torque-steer problems even with moderate power outputs.

This layout has been adopted almost universally by European car manufacturers for smaller cars since the late

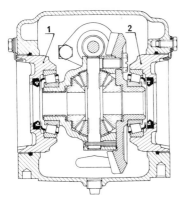

Fig. 2.19. Renault 5 differential bearing adjusting rings—these ring nuts, (1) and (2), and locking plates provide the differential bearing adjustment

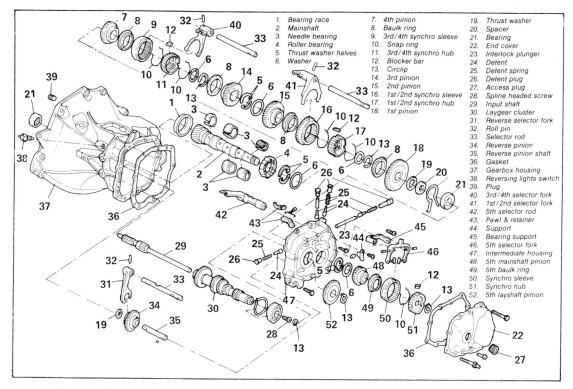

1.	Bearing race	7.	4th pinion	19.	Thrust washer
2.	Mainshaft	8.	Baulk ring	20.	Spacer
3.	Needle bearing	9.	3rd/4th synchro sleeve	21.	Bearing
4.	Roller bearing	10.	Snap ring	22.	End cover
5.	Thrust washer halves	11.	3rd/4th synchro hub	23.	Interlock plunger
6.	Washer	12.	Blocker bar	24.	Detent
		13.	Circlip	25.	Detent spring
		14.	3rd pinion	26.	Detent plug
		15.	2nd pinion	27.	Access plug
		16.	1st/2nd synchro sleeve	28.	Spline headed screw
		17.	1st/2nd synchro hub	29.	Input shaft
		18.	1st pinion	30.	Laygear cluster

31. Reverse selector fork
32. Roll pin
33. Selector rod
34. Reverse pinion
35. Reverse pinion shaft
36. Gasket
37. Gearbox housing
38. Reversing lights switch
39. Plug
40. 3rd/4th selector fork
41. 1st/2nd selector fork
42. 5th selector rod
43. Pawl & retainer
44. Support
45. Bearing support
46. 5th selector fork
47. Intermediate housing
48. 5th mainshaft pinion
49. 5th baulk ring
50. Synchro sleeve
51. Synchro hub
52. 5th layshaft pinion

1970s due to its extremely good space utilization and economy of parts.

The particular design used by Vauxhall has the clever additional feature of allowing the clutch to be changed without removing the gearbox.

The Astra uses a single-dry-plate diaphragm spring clutch actuated by a cable. The clutch is mounted in an alloy housing between the engine and gearbox, which has a removable lower cover (Fig. 2.21). Power is taken to the gearbox by a splined shaft, which is not simply an extension of the gearbox input shaft, but is a splined sliding fit within it, allowing the shaft to be withdrawn from the clutch for clutch removal. The shaft is withdrawn with a special puller via a plug in the gearbox end cover (Fig. 2.22).

Apart from being hollow, as described above, the gearbox input shaft is of the same design as those used on other all-indirect gearboxes and carries the fixed gear

Fig. 2.20. The Vauxhall Astra transmission layout is a very modern, compact, transverse, front-wheel-drive layout

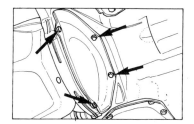

Fig. 2.21. The Astra clutch/gearbox design allows easy clutch removal

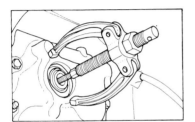

Fig. 2.22. Withdrawing the Astra clutch spigot shaft to free the clutch assembly

wheels. The synchronizer hubs and free gears are mounted on the output shaft, below and behind the input shaft. The five-speed gearboxes, where fitted, are the same as the four-speed gearboxes with the exception of an additional gear pair and synchronizer mounted beyond the gearbox end web.in an enlarged end cover, just as on the Renault 5.

The helical spur final drive pinion is mounted at the engine end of the output shaft and drives the bevel gear differential, which sits behind the gearbox, towards the engine, in the one-piece clutch/gearbox/differential casing. The differential bearing preload is adjustable by a threaded bearing adjuster ring in the outboard side of the differential casing, but the final drive mesh is fixed during manufacture.

Birfield-type constant velocity joints are used at both ends of the unequal-length solid driveshafts.

The overall arrangement reduces the number of drivetrain components required to an absolute minimum for greater economy and also reliablity.

8) Four-wheel-drive: Land Rover

Land Rover's range of four-wheel-drive vehicles has a unique transmission layout, which is common to the whole range (Fig. 2.23). The transmission not only provides for the transfer of power to all four wheels, but also, on some models, has auxiliary power take-off points to drive external equipment.

The engine, either diesel or petrol, is mounted inline at the front of the vehicle and transmits power through a conventional single-plate dry clutch to the gearbox. As far as the output shaft the gearbox, too, is of conventional construction, with the power input going to the four-speed three-synchro mainshaft sitting above the layshaft in the casing. Gears one to three are indirect, i.e. the power is transmitted via the layshaft, but fourth gear is direct and therefore of 1:1 ratio.

Mounted on the rear of the gearbox casing, where the tailshaft casing would be on a conventional gearbox, is the transfer box. This transfers drive from the gearbox to the two propshafts, one for each driven axle, and contains the mechanism for the low range gearing and selection of two-

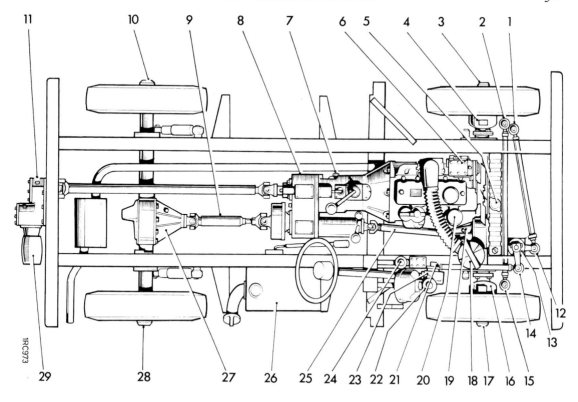

1RC973

Fig. 2.23. The transmission layout of the Land Rover—built for neither speed nor comfort

or four-wheel drive. An idler shaft carrying a two-wheel idler gear sits between the input and output shafts, the latter carrying a sliding low ratio transfer gear, which can either be slid into mesh with the rear wheel of the idler or forward to link the high transfer gear to the output shaft by means of a dog clutch.

The output shaft runs back to the rear propshaft and forward, through the four-wheel-drive selection dog clutch, to the front propshaft. The rear propshaft is thus always engaged, but the front may be disengaged for road use. This arrangement contrasts with modern, albeit higher performance and road use oriented, four-wheel-drive transmissions, which provide a third centre differential and hence can benefit from permanently engaged four-wheel drive, without tyre scrubbing, on all surfaces.

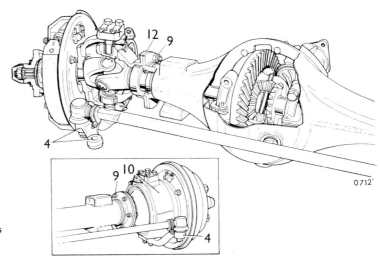

Fig. 2.24. The Land Rover front axle showing the universal joints located on the steering king pin axes

The rear of the transfer box carries the transmission parking brake acting on all four wheels, if in four-wheel drive, or on both rears otherwise.

The propshafts incorporating Hooke's type universal joints carry the drive to the front and rear live axles. The rear axle is of conventional construction, but the front axle (Fig. 2.24) differs from it at the outer ends by having the steering hub king pins mounted on an extension of the axle outer casing. The steering deflection is accommodated in the halfshafts by a single Hooke's joint at the outer ends mounted on the king pin axis.

These, despite experiencing great angular movement due to the steering, are not constant velocity joints (chapter 6), but smoothness of drive is less important than robustness and ease of repair in a vehicle of this type.

Chapter 3 | Clutches

As mentioned earlier on in chapter 1, a clutch is a mechanism which enables the rotation of one shaft to be transmitted to, or disconnected from, a second shaft running on the same axis. The clutch in any passenger car is of the gradual engagement type whereby torque from the engine can be transmitted *progressively* to the gearbox in order to provide jolt-free take-up of drive. Three basic methods are used to transmit drive in clutches and these are friction, magnetism and hydraulic action, of which the friction method is by far the most common in cars with manual transmissions, and the only type with which we are concerned in this chapter.

Friction clutches

Friction clutches fall into more than one category, with cone clutches (very early devices on motor cars), single-plate, multi-plate, wet multi-plate and centrifugal clutches being the fundamental types. In dealing with light vehicles of the last 30 years or so, however, we are likely to come across two basic designs, both of which are single-plate, dry clutches. The earlier type is rarely seen on modern motor cars although many heavy commercial vehicles still use it. It is the coil spring type (Fig. 3.1) with release levers or *fingers*. The later (current) type, which has in fact been in use since the mid-1960s, is the diaphragm spring clutch (Fig. 3.2) which uses one circular band of spring steel as the clamping spring rather than a series of coil springs.

In the coil spring clutch, clamping pressure between flywheel and pressure plate surfaces is provided by a series of coil springs disposed in a circle concentric with the clutch plate; there are usually at least six springs, and often

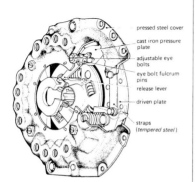

pressed steel cover

cast iron pressure plate

adjustable eye bolts

eye bolt fulcrum pins

release lever

driven plate

straps (tempered steel)

Fig. 3.1. A sectioned multi-coil spring clutch

Fig. 3.2. This is an exploded view of a typical diaphragm spring clutch; the release bearing, lever and flywheel are shown 'ghosted'. This particular assembly is from the Chrysler Avenger

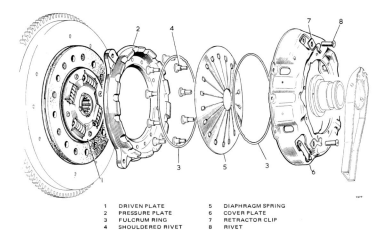

1	DRIVEN PLATE	5	DIAPHRAGM SPRING
2	PRESSURE PLATE	6	COVER PLATE
3	FULCRUM RING	7	RETRACTOR CLIP
4	SHOULDERED RIVET	8	RIVET

many more. Referring to Fig. 3.3, it can be seen that the springs are located between the pressed steel clutch cover and the cast-iron pressure plate. Straps made from spring steel are used to transmit the drive from the cover to the pressure plate, while release levers, which pivot on fulcrum pins supported in adjustable eye bolts, connect the release lever thrust plate to small struts positioned between the lever and the pressure plate. The efficiency of the release mechanism is aided by these struts and, along with the driving straps, they allow the pressure plate to move smoothly, thus avoiding clutch judder.

The clutch cover assembly is bolted to the engine flywheel and as its mounting bolts are tightened the axial coil springs are compressed, so that the pressure plate is forced against the clutch plate which is in turn forced against the flywheel face. Thus the clutch assembly forms one solid coupling through which torque can be transmitted from the flywheel to the gearbox input shaft. This shaft is splined to the centre of the clutch plate. By applying an axial force on the release thrust plate, however, the release levers are pushed in and their pivoting action forces the clutch cover away from the flywheel, thus decompressing the coil springs and reducing the clamping force progressively until it is zero. This is how the clutch is disengaged. It is probably easier to comprehend this action by studying the construction of the Morris Minor's clutch in Fig. 3.3. The release levers are usually individually

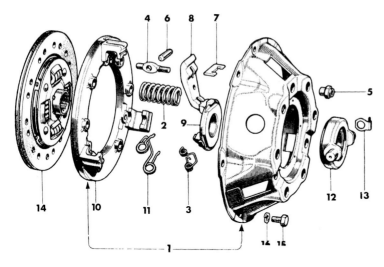

1.   Clutch assembly
2.   Thrust spring
3.   Release lever retainer
4.   Eyebolt
5.   Eyebolt nut
6.   Release lever pin
7.   Strut
8.   Release lever
9.   Bearing thrust plate
10. Pressure plate
11. Anti-rattle spring
12. Release bearing
13. Retainer
14. Driven plate assembly
15. Clutch to flywheel screw
16. Spring washer

Fig. 3.3. Exploded view of the Morris Minor coil spring clutch assembly

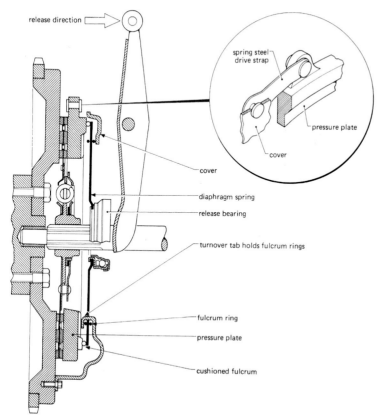

Fig. 3.4. A cross-section through a diaphragm spring clutch; note the fulcrum ring about which the diaphragm spring pivots

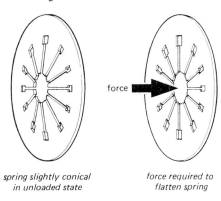

spring slightly conical
in unloaded state

force required to
flatten spring

Fig. 3.5. The normally concave form of the diaphragm spring is flattened when the release bearing pushes against it

adjustable to ensure even movement for a given amount of thrust plate travel; the effect of imbalanced adjustment of the levers is clutch judder, directly caused by uneven contact pressure between clutch plate and pressure plate/flywheel faces.

The modern diaphragm clutch (Fig. 3.4) works in a very similar manner but the spring action of the diaphragm replaces that of the coil springs in the previous type. This type has no release levers, however, and so no lever adjustment. The diaphragm is a circular band of spring steel which is dished (Fig. 3.5); if the dish shape is flattened the diaphragm exerts an axial force in either direction. As the clutch cover is screwed down to the flywheel it flattens the diaphragm and so a clamping force is caused on the clutch plate. With a fulcrum ring positioned radially about the diaphragm as in Fig. 3.4, the effect of pushing the centre of the diaphragm band inwards is to buckle it up, so causing its outer edge (connected to the pressure plate) to move outwards; thus clutch disengagement is achieved.

The release mechanism
On both coil spring and diaphragm clutches, the axial disengagement force is provided by a release bearing which is moved by the release mechanism and controlled by the clutch pedal. The release bearing not only pushes on the diaphragm centre or thrust plate but also has to spin with this when the engine is running: until a few years ago this bearing was in the form of a carbon ring which simply slides against the surface of the thrust plate but this has mostly been replaced by the ball-race-type thrust bearing (a ball-race bearing capable of taking axial rather than radial loads).

Ball-race bearings can be checked for wear by separating the two race halves and checking for pitting or breaking of the hardened surfaces (if of the type that can be dismantled) or else by simply spinning in the hand and feeling for roughness. Fig. 3.6 shows a typical ball-race release bearing; it is of the unretained type and so merely sits on the release lever. Note the shiny areas on the lever, which indicate moving contact with the bearing: such areas should be kept lightly greased.

Fig. 3.6. The clutch housing, release lever and bearing from a Peugeot 305; the release lever pivots on a ball joint and is held to it by a spring-steel clip

Carbon ring bearings wear visibly and the height of the carbon ring itself is a good indication of how much wear has occurred. Clutch release bearings of both the carbon ring and ball types should ideally be replaced as a matter of course when a clutch is being renewed.

An interesting alternative execution to the conventional release bearing layout is the one employed in larger-engined Volkswagen Golf models (Fig. 5.1, chapter 5) where the clutch release lever is situated at the opposite end of the gearbox from the clutch and thrusts on a long rod which runs the length of the hollow mainshaft, and to the centre of the clutch. This clutch assembly is also unusual for being 'the wrong way around', that is, the pressure plate/diaphragm is bolted to the crankshaft, and the flywheel is mounted to it in turn.

Release mechanisms fall into two common categories: hydraulic and cable types. On early cars a rod linkage was employed to relay pedal movement to the release bearing but this was soon made obsolete because of its complexity

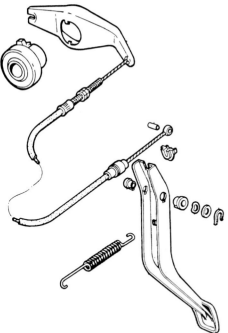

and the problems caused by movement of the power unit. Cable actuation tends to be favoured more and more these days as it is reliable, simple and cheap, although hydraulic release mechanisms are still widespread and more suited to installations where a clutch cable would have to follow a tortuous path.

Clutch cables (Fig. 3.7 shows a typical cable layout) tend to last a long time but if one has already provided long service it is wise to renew it for the sake of reliability. Cable problems are few and tend to be obvious: stretching of the inner cable will result in a reduced margin of adjustment (if a screw adjuster is fitted at one end) and lack of lubrication will manifest itself as notchy, stiff clutch pedal movement. If the inner cable can be removed from its outer sheath (which is not often the case) then it should also be checked for fraying. Pumping grease into the outer cable, or removing the inner and smearing it, is not a procedure often recommended by the car manufacturer but in our opinion it can do more good than harm.

Hydraulic release mechanisms (see the typical arrangement shown in Fig. 3.8) suffer exactly the same problems

Above **Fig. 3.7. The components of the Ford Cortina's cable-type clutch release mechanism**

Right **Fig. 3.8. The hydraulic release mechanism comprises a master cylinder, high-pressure piping and slave cylinder to operate the clutch release lever**

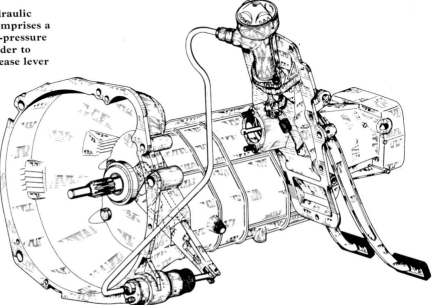

as braking system hydraulics as they work in the same manner and are executed in just the same way. The biggest enemy is internal corrosion of the master or slave cylinder bore, causing seal failure and this is usually due to water-contaminated hydraulic fluid—the result of infrequent fluid changes. Any leaks in the hydraulic piping, be it steel, plastic or rubber piping, will cause eventual, if not immediate, loss of clutch actuation. A leaking master cylinder seal will cause 'creep', whereby initial application of the pedal disengages the clutch, but sustained pedal pressure fails to maintain total disengagement and worsening *clutch drag* occurs—a condition whereby complete disengagement cannot be achieved. A leaking slave cylinder seal can generate the same symptom and will often only allow partial disengagement of the clutch. Re-sealing of master or slave cylinders is not recommended and either should be renewed if malfunctioning.

It should be mentioned that a certain amount of free play is usually required in a release mechanism, whether it is of the cable or hydraulic type, and where play is specified it is important to set it correctly if release bearing/diaphragm fingers/thrust plate wear is to be avoided and full clutch spring thrust is to act on the pressure plate. As the clutch plate lining wears, the clearance decreases, so unless periodic adjustment is made, the clearance will disappear altogether and the clutch will start to *slip*. Certain cars, such as the Mini, are adjustable not only for free play, but also for total clutch 'throw' or travel. It is even more important to ensure that the 'throw' setting is correct, as if too much throw is allowed this can cause the engine crankshaft to be pushed axially every time the clutch pedal is depressed, thus generating crankshaft thrust washer wear. Other designs of clutch mechanism (such as on certain older GM models) are specially spring loaded to maintain permanent contact between thrust (release) bearing and clutch assembly, while all modern European Fords have a self-compensating (self-adjusting) cable using a one-way ratchet adjuster at the pedal (A, Fig. 3.9), which distinguishes itself on Fiestas by slipping from time to time with a resounding crash. Only your workshop manual can help establish which type your car has.

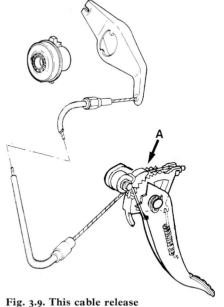

Fig. 3.9. This cable release mechanism features a wear compensator in the form of a pawl and ratchet (A) at the top of the pedal. It is a Ford design

Fig. 3.10. The release lever joint should be kept clean and greased

Needless to say, any friction in the moving parts of a clutch release mechanism is unwelcome and should be eliminated. All clutch pedal and release fork lever joints should be kept clean and greased (Fig. 3.10) and should be checked for wear. The ball joint at the base of the Mini's (i.e. most Leyland 'gears-in-sump') clutch release lever is prone to wear due to its exposure to road dirt: this often leads to inadequate clutch release travel and insufficient disengagement. Ball-type or through-pin pivots on release forks located inside the clutch housing are best lubricated with a high-temperature metal-loaded grease such as Copaslip.

Clutch problems

The clutch in every car equipped with manual transmission takes a hammering in everyday use. Because it is designed to progressively transmit torque it is by necessity designed to disperse energy in the form of heat when it is neither fully engaged nor fully disengaged, but in a state of slip. As the clutch must be smooth in operation for the sake of comfort, the friction plate is made of a relatively soft material (mostly asbestos) and so its surface wears each time it is engaged or disengaged and forced to slip. Because of this the friction disc or *clutch plate* has a limited life and is one of the 'consumable' components of the car along with the brake linings and exhaust system. Its longevity is determined by the driving style of the car's driver, and by the torque characteristics and overall gearing of the car: a large-engined vehicle producing a lot of torque at fairly low engine speeds will need less clutch slip or *clutch riding* when pulling away than will a less powerful car that develops most of its torque at, say, 4000 rpm. The longevity can be impaired by a badly adjusted release mechanism. Thus one car can still have its original clutch plate working satisfactorily after 50,000 miles of use while another can require a new plate after a mere 20,000 miles.

Because of the amount of slip that a clutch assembly can be subjected to, the energy that it dissipates in the form of heat can be quite significant and so the clutch can become very hot. Excessive heat can cause scorching of the clutch plate linings, distortion of the plate, and blueing, cracking and distortion of the flywheel and pressure plate faces. When a clutch plate is worn out it tends to slip, even when engaged, and this is due to the reduced thickness of the plate causing the clutch spring(s) to deflect towards their unstressed position, thereby reducing the clamping force on the plate. Such slip can become so acute that it results in a 'burn-out' where the plate actually starts to 'cook', clouds of acrid smoke emanate from the engine compartment and all drive is lost. Of course, this can cause damage to more than the friction plate itself.

Another problem that commonly manifests itself when a clutch plate is excessively worn, is *clutch drag*, where, with the clutch pedal fully depressed and the release mechanism correctly adjusted, the clutch does not fully disengage. This condition, which causes stiff gear selection and often impossible engagement of reverse gear, can be due to insufficient release lever travel, sticky clutch mating faces, catching of the friction plate on the input shaft (or primary drive) splines, or just a worn plate.

Checking the clutch assembly

The basic clutch friction plate (Fig. 3.11) comprises splined central hub, hub plates, torsional damping springs, crimp-plate and the friction linings, plus the rivets which hold it all together. When inspecting a clutch plate

**Fig. 3.11. Typical construction of
a clutch friction plate**

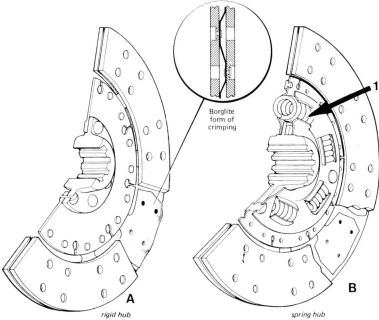

Borglite
form of
crimping

1

A

rigid hub

B

spring hub

assembly it is important to be aware of the following
points:

1. Torsional damping springs (1, Fig. 3.11) which appear
   loose in the hub plates are designed to be so; usually it is
   only one or two that are loose and this is because the
   springs are of different rates. The springs serve to absorb
   jolts as drive is taken up and not all cars have them. Some
   cars, such as the earlier Mini and its brethren, have no
   springs and therefore incorporate no torsional damping.
   A rigid hub clutch plate is shown at A, Fig. 3.11.
2. Radial channels in the friction linings (Fig. 3.12) are not
   primarily wear indicators but dust extractors and an aid
   to plate cooling. However, if the channels are nearly
   worn away, you can be pretty sure that the time has come
   to change the clutch plate. The best judge of the degree
   of lining wear is the remaining depth of the lining rivet
   holes: if this is 2 mm or less then you should discard the
   plate, as exposed rivet heads will permanently damage
   the flywheel face. Something you will invariably notice
   about the wear of the linings is that it is greater on one
   side of the plate than the other. This is because the

Fig. 3.12. These dust-extracting radial channels in the friction material are also a good guide to wear

flywheel is hotter than the pressure plate (due to absorbing heat directly from the crankshaft) and thus causes accelerated lining wear.

3. When the clutch plate is viewed edge-on, the gap which is apparent between the linings is due to crimping (kinking or waving) of the thin plates upon which the lining material is mounted (inset, A, Fig. 3.11). This crimping serves to cushion clamping jolts as the clutch is engaged. The resulting air space between the linings also helps cooling.

4. The lining material itself should not be cracked, have chunks missing out of it, or be burnt. A burnt lining can be smelt, but also looks dark brown or black, although invariably not uniformly so. If burning is evident, this may testify to overheating caused by slip or riding the clutch, or else to oil contamination from either the gearbox front or crankshaft rear oil seal. If either symptom is present, the clutch plate should be renewed. Checking the linings for trueness is advisable as warping can cause clutch drag: the check can be carried out with a steel rule and feeler gauges as detailed for the pressure plate and flywheel later.

5. Loose rivets anywhere on the plate assembly should not be tolerated; one or two loose rivets can often safely be tightened by a judicious tap with a centre punch.

6. The condition of the splines in the centre hub (Fig. 3.13) is of paramount importance to the good functioning of

Fig. 3.13. Make sure that the splines in the centre hub of the friction plate are free from greasy asbestos dust and are undamaged. This Peugeot plate has a particularly large hub opening as it fits over the primary drive gear in a front-wheel-drive application, rather than the narrow-diameter input shaft of an inline gearbox

the clutch. Examined under a bright light, the splines should be square edged, parallel and free of burrs. There should be no rust on or between them and dirt, such as greasy asbestos dust, should be removed. Minor burrs and light rust can be removed with a fine file. The same conditions apply to the splines of the gearbox input shaft or primary drive gear.

7. When refitting the clutch plate, make sure that it goes on to the input shaft facing the correct way: your manual will tell you which direction this is and will refer to the side with the raised hub or the 'FLYWHEEL FACE' marking.

The coil springs or diaphragm spring of a clutch rarely give any problems, although if they have been used for a very high mileage then they can be expected to have weakened somewhat and to have lost some clamping force. High-mileage coil springs should ideally be renewed if the car is being restored, as should the diaphragm spring of later cars (usually supplied as one item with the clutch cover). Where a diaphragm spring is slotted at its centre to produce *fingers* (Fig. 3.14), check the surface of these fingers at the point where they are contacted by the release bearing (usually their very tips—arrowed, Fig. 3.14). This part will be polished but should not be worn to the extent

Fig. 3.14. The polished tips of these diaphragm fingers are still usable but will be giving problems in about 10,000 miles!

that a pronounced groove has been eroded; wear of the fingers is by no means uncommon and often results in total loss of clutch disengagement as the finger ends break off and the release bearing pushes through the centre of the diaphragm. On coil-spring-type clutches with release levers, check the pivoting ends of the levers, including any bushings and pivot pins and also the eye bolts for wear (steps or ridges, not just polishing)—see Figs. 3.2 and 3.3. Replace individual components where necessary, if these can be obtained separately.

If the clutch is known to judder or you wish to check for this condition, the flywheel face, clutch plate and pressure plate should first be visually checked for oil contamination or discolouration due to overheating. Distortion of the flywheel or pressure plate is best checked with an accurate straight-edged instrument such as a good quality steel rule, in conjunction with feeler gauges. Laying the rule diametrically across each in turn, look first for areas under the rule where there appears to be no contact with the mating face being checked and then verify the trueness by trying to slide a 0.10 mm feeler gauge between rule and face at various points (Fig. 3.15). If the feeler can slide under at any point then there is clearly distortion, and although the flywheel or pressure plate can probably be machined true by an engineering works, it is preferable to renew it as the

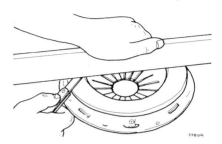

Fig. 3.15. An accurate straight-edge and feeler gauges are all that are needed to check the trueness of this pressure plate

Fig. 3.16. This flywheel face is sufficiently scored to shorten the life of the friction plate. The future mileage expectations of the car will determine whether it is worth machining the face, renewing the flywheel or just putting things back together and letting sleeping dogs lie!

removal of metal will impair the heat-sinking properties of the components. Distortion across any of the mating faces causes clutch judder, although apparent judder can also be caused by worn or loose engine mountings.

Scoring of the flywheel or pressure plate surfaces (Fig. 3.16) often occurs when the clutch plate has been allowed to wear down excessively, thus exposing its rivet heads, but it can also be caused (more rarely) by abrasive grit being caught between the components. Scoring is undesirable as it shortens the life of the clutch plate linings, but it can be tolerated if only light. Heavier scoring can be remedied by having the affected faces skimmed.

When a clutch assembly is fitted to the flywheel (or to the pressure plate, depending upon the particular design) the clutch plate must be aligned axially with the spigot bearing (or the primary drive gear on power units with a gearbox *under* the engine) before the clutch cover bolts are fully tightened. It is not usually sufficient to align the assembly by eye so a stepped mandrel (Fig. 3.18) is often employed for the job. This is basically a rod which is a tight fit in the spigot bearing and also in the clutch centre hub, and when it is pushed through both to align them, the clutch cover bolts can be tightened to their full torque and the mandrel removed. On installations with drop gears, where the gearbox shafts run parallel to the crankshaft, the clutch plate locates on the splines of the *primary drive gear*, which component is located on the crankshaft nose. On some such arrangements (and the notorious Mini features here, and Peugeot 204/304/305 models), the flywheel, clutch plate and pressure plate can be fitted over the primary drive/crankshaft nose before final tightening, thus allowing the clutch plate to be aligned on the gear before being firmly 'sandwiched'. The original diaphragm-type Borg & Beck Mini clutch assembly is shown in Fig. 2.14.

Finally, it is worth mentioning that most clutch assemblies are balanced with the engine at the factory to ensure smooth, vibration-free running. Some clutch covers are marked for alignment with the flywheel but if no mark is apparent then make your own before removal and ensure that the assembly is refitted in exactly the same angular relationship (Fig. 3.9). Some clutches can only be

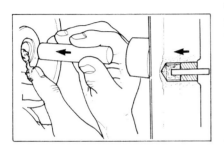

Fig. 3.17. Removing a spigot bush by hydraulic ejection

Left **Fig. 3.18.** A clutch plate
alignment mandrel; the small-
diameter end fits snugly in the
spigot bearing while the two
bushes on the shaft are a tight
fit through the centre hub of two
different clutch plates. The
tapered knob at the right-hand
side is purely a handle

Below **Fig. 3.19.** Aligning the
clutch assembly

fitted in one position anyway, due to the spacing of the
retaining bolts or else the presence of a locating dowel or
two.

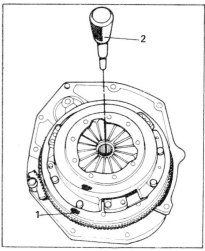

1. Painted balance marks 2. Aligning tool

Chapter 4 | Gearbox overhaul

Fig. 4.1. Rawlbolts; the outer sleeve expands as the bolt is tightened

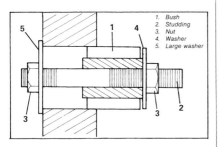

1. Bush
2. Studding
3. Nut
4. Washer
5. Large washer

Fig. 4.2. A simple bush installation tool can be made up from a length of studding (or a set screw), two nuts and suitably sized washers

Working methods

When working on transmission systems there are a handful of problems which are regularly encountered, other than interference and shrink fits, which are covered later.

If, for instance, a bearing outer race cannot be easily removed by prying out with screwdrivers, then a handy trick is to fit a Rawlbolt (an expanding masonry bolt—see Fig. 4.1) of nearly the same internal diameter into it, screw the bolt in to expand its outer sleeve, and pull the race by virtue of the Rawlbolt sleeve's grip. This method can be used on all sorts of bushes and cups in blind locations as Rawlbolts are available in many different diameters. It can also be used as an alternative method of removal for spigot bearings.

Heating components to expand them in the hope that they will ease their grip on bearings, bushes and tracks usually works effectively, but care must be taken not to overheat light alloy castings as these can distort permanently. Judicious use of a blowtorch on steel and cast-iron components is usually all right, but heating of aluminium should only be effected by hot, wet rags or immersion in hot water.

Presses can often be improvised using washers and a nut and bolt as shown in Fig. 4.2, where tightening of the bolt will pull a bearing or a race into its housing. This is preferable to using a hammer and drift for the job as the bearing suffers no impacting. By using a suitable spacer to brace one end of the tool against the surrounding housing, it is also possible to remove the bearing.

If a bearing is being levered out of a housing bore or off a shaft, you should always ensure that pressure is applied to it evenly around its circumference as it will otherwise be forced askew and will jam. If a bearing (or any component for that matter) is being levered out, it is better to lever it with two same-sized levers positioned at 180 degrees to each other. While doing this it often helps to tap the component from which it is being levered, in the opposite direction, even if it cannot apparently move.

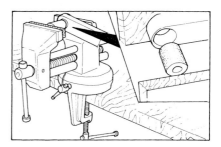

Above **Fig. 4.3. A vice may be used to press a component into a tight surround**

Don't be tempted to drift transmission components into or out of place with steel drifts—brass or wooden drifts should always be used in preference. Of course it is permissible to drift bearings using steel sockets of suitable diameter, but only if excessive force is not needed, and only if the drift socket is in contact with the bearing track which is gripping (i.e. the outer track if in a housing, or the inner track if on a shaft). It is also possible to press some components into a tight location with the aid of a G-clamp or vice (Fig. 4.3).

When dealing with circlips (of which there are many different types) do not be tempted to prize them out of place with screwdrivers if you don't have the right circlip pliers; this action nearly always results in a permanently damaged circlip and does not solve the problem of fitting the new clip when the time comes. It is not usually necessary to renew a circlip, but if there is ANY suspicion that it has been bent upon removal then it MUST be replaced. This same thinking also applies to roll pins, although these tend to be quite tough.

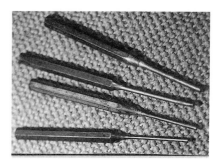

Above **Fig. 4.4. Pin punches are square-ended and available in many diameters**

When driving a roll pin from its location, always use a square-ended drift (ideally a pin punch), as an implement with a tapered end will splay the pin outwards, thus increasing its grip.

If you encounter an oil seal to which it is impossible to gain access from behind for the purpose of removal, it can be pulled out with the aid of one or more self-tapping screws screwed into its surface (Fig. 4.5). When installing an oil seal, be sure to tap it into place squarely and unless specific fitting instructions are given, push it in as far as any visible shoulder in its housing, or else tap it in just flush with the front face of the housing.

Collect all components in various containers such as yoghurt pots and label them clearly, especially if you're not

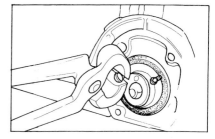

Fig. 4.5. If an oil seal is fitted flush with a housing and cannot be attained from its inside diameter, then screw some self-tappers into it and pull on them with pincers or pliers

going to reassemble for a few weeks, as you'll never remember what went where! It can often pay in the long run to make notes or sketches of the assembly of parts as you strip them because there are some mysteries that even an exploded diagram in a workshop manual can't solve.

Any holes or galleries in housings and shafts should (once the component has been thoroughly cleaned) be poked through with wire to ensure that they are not obstructed. Blind bolt and stud holes should be free from oil, water or cleaning fluid before being used, as a hydraulic lock can cause damage on tightening the relevant fastening.

The first stage in any gearbox overhaul is the removal, cleaning and stripping of the gearbox. While the procedure for doing this will vary a lot in detail with the particular gearbox design, all the commonly encountered methods are covered in this section.

When the gearbox has been removed from the car (consult your workshop manual regarding this), it must be cleaned thoroughly to prevent dirt and grit from the exterior of the gearbox contaminating the internal components. If the power unit is of the gearbox-in-sump type, the gearbox should be left attached to the engine during cleaning. Before starting to clean, any holes through to the inside of the gearbox, such as the exits for the speedometer drive cable and the propshaft or driveshafts, should be plugged with suitable plastic caps, if available, or wads of kitchen paper. If using paper, take care that no small pieces become detached when removing the plugs after cleaning, as these can block any oilways in the gearbox (or engine if of the gearbox-in-sump type).

Older gearbox casings were made of cast iron, but newer ones take advantage of the reduced weight of aluminium alloy castings. Particularly with alloy casings, care should be taken with the fasteners securing the casings or cover plates, as the threads in the casings can strip very easily. Any external linkages on the gearbox casing should be removed and their position and adjustment carefully noted before dismantling the casing.

Whatever the layout of the gearbox, three main approaches exist to the casing design and disassembly. Casings are either in one piece with cast-alloy, pressed steel or plastic cover plates to allow access (Fig. 4.6) or are made in two or more separable sections. Multiple section casings separate into either longitudinal sections (Fig. 4.7) or into lateral sections (Fig. 4.8), usually halves. Cover plates on the first type of casing are retained by set screws or bolts, possibly with locating dowels, while multiple section casings are more often held together by studs. Do not remove studs for the sake of it as the likelihood of damage to the casing will be increased. Fasteners from different components should, as mentioned previously, be kept separately, yoghurt pots being ideal for the purpose, and if there is any chance of confusing fasteners from the same component, they may be pushed through or attached to a piece of card marked with the outline of the components in their respective positions. Gaskets from the gearbox should be retained in case a replacement has to be fabricated using the old one as a pattern. The positions of any O-rings between casing sections for the purposes of oil supply should be noted, as failure to replace these will result in serious oil leaks or loss of oil pressure with a pressurized lubrication system.

The order of disassembly of the gearbox internals will also vary significantly from one gearbox to another. In some cases, the selector mechanism will already have been removed by this stage with the gearbox top cover, such as in the Jaguar Mk 2 in chapter 2, while other designs will require the removal of the selectors next before the shafts

Fig. 4.6. One-piece casing construction on the Renault 5

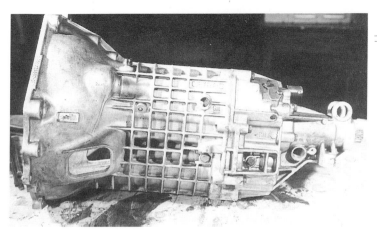

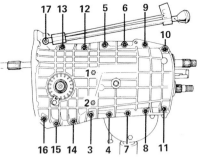

Above Fig. 4.7. Longitudinally-split casing on the Renault 18, showing the tightening sequence for casing bolts

Left Fig. 4.8. Vauxhall Carlton Getrag gearbox showing the laterally-split casing or vice versa. Typical methods for the removal of these components are described below and a close look at the gearbox being dismantled should reveal which should be removed first.

Disassembly of selectors

Selector mechanisms, if not housed in a cover plate, run on shafts in the gearbox casing(s) parallel to the mainshaft (Fig. 4.9). If the gearbox is a transverse installation there may also be a shaft or shafts running perpendicular to the mainshaft from the external gear linkage. The interlock mechanism, preventing simultaneous selection of more than one gear, will be on these shafts. If it is not necessary to remove the selector mechanism then this can be left in place and the job of selector reassembly avoided. Interlock mechanisms in many gearboxes consist of sprung plungers between the shafts allowing enough room for only one of the selector shafts to move at a time. The selector mechanism may also incorporate detent plungers, also acting on the selector shafts (Fig. 4.10). These plungers are often removed by releasing a screw cap covering the plunger bore to gain access to the plungers. A magnetic probe can be used to retrieve plungers left in the bore, if they do not come out with the springs (Fig. 4.11). All the

Fig. 4.9. Selector shafts and forks in a Peugeot 305 gearbox

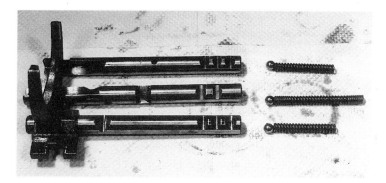

Left **Fig. 4.10. Detent balls and selector rods from Peugeot 305 gearbox**

Above **Fig. 4.11. Using a magnetic probe to remove interlock plungers from a Getrag gearbox**

Below **Fig. 4.12. Sleeve-type interlock device from the Mini and Leyland transverse gearbox**

components must be collected and kept in order for reassembly. An alternative mechanism on the Mini (Fig. 4.12) uses a sliding collar concentric to the interlock input shaft from the gear lever to prevent it engaging with more than one of the individual selector shafts. Usually the interlock mechanism is removed first, allowing sufficient motion of the selector shafts for them to be removed entirely from the casing, possibly after also loosening the selector forks from the shafts by undoing a clamp bolt or roll pin, if present (Fig. 4.13).

In other designs the selector shafts are fixed positively in the casing and the selector forks are a sliding fit on the selector shafts. In this case the fastener locating the selector shaft, often a set screw, roll pin or cover plate, must be removed to free the selector shaft. Selector and interlock designs vary greatly and ideally a workshop manual should be consulted for detailed disassembly.

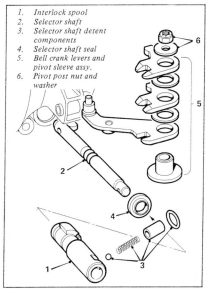

1. Interlock spool
2. Selector shaft
3. Selector shaft detent components
4. Selector shaft seal
5. Bell crank levers and pivot sleeve assy.
6. Pivot post nut and washer

Left **Fig. 4.13. Drifting roll pin retainer from Peugeot 305 selector fork**

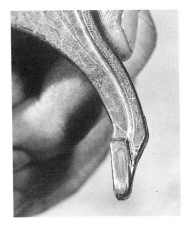

Above **Fig. 4.14. Surface of Peugeot 305 selector fork showing minimal amount of wear**

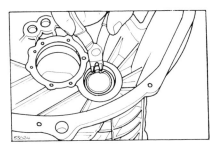

Above **Fig. 4.15. Removal of circlip retainer from Getrag layshaft bearing**

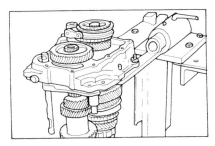

Above **Fig. 4.16. Laterally-split casing showing access to shafts before bearing removal on the Vauxhall Astra**

The selector shafts and interlock components should not show any wear on their sliding surfaces. If they do, they should be replaced, as this can cause stiffness in the gearchange. The bores in which the shafts run should also be inspected to ensure they contain no grit or swarf, as this is another common cause of a stiff gearchange. The selector forks will usually show some wear on their sides where they come into contact with the synchronizers (Fig. 4.14). Scuffing or polishing of the selectors is not serious, but deep scoring of the surfaces shows that they need replacements. If this is found, also inspect the corresponding surfaces on the synchronizers for excess wear, judged by the same criterion.

Disassembly of gearbox shafts

The method of removal of the gearbox gears, shafts and bearings depends to some extent on the construction of the gearbox casing. Where the casing is one-piece, the bearings and shafts may be retained by half caps or, more commonly, by internal or external circlips in the end flanges of the casing (Fig. 4.15). Where the casing splits into longitudinal sections, the same circlip method is often used, but the shafts are accessible on separation of the casing sections, before the bearings have been removed (Fig. 4.16). With a transversely split casing the bearings and shafts are freed simply by splitting the casing halves (Fig. 4.17). It may be necessary to undo any nuts on the outer ends of the shafts to allow their removal, particularly where the bearings are retained in the gearbox end webs in a one-piece casing. These nuts will usually be locked by a lock tab or a staking extension, which should be knocked or levered back before the nut can be loosened (Fig. 4.18). If the interlock mechanism has been removed the shafts can be locked by manually moving the selector forks or synchronizers to select two gears at once (Fig. 4.19), while undoing the nuts. The interlock mechanism is often removed at this stage expressly to facilitate the locking of the shafts.

Bearings retained by a half cap are freed by removing the cap, usually retained by bolts or studs. Bearings retained in casing flanges require the removal of the internal or external circlip retaining them and then pulling or drifting from the flange (Fig. 4.20). Access to drift a bearing from a flange is often limited by the components on the shaft. When drifting the bearing it is important to ensure that the drift is placed on the bearing outer race, unless specifically stated to the contrary by the manual. Drifting the inner race can cause damage to the bearing due to the high impact loading. The drift should be blunt ended and should be moved around the bearing to ensure even movement on all sides. As the bearing moves up its bore, be careful that the drift does not damage the sides, as this can make the casing unusable. If hitting the shaft is permissible a hide- or copper-faced mallet should be used (Fig. 4.21) but never a steel-faced hammer as this can damage the shaft. If there is insufficient travel to drift the bearing from the flange, due to the components on the shaft fouling the flange, then it will be necessary to drift it out in several stages. This can be done by tapping the shaft back through the bearing and interposing a suitably shaped spacer piece between the end of the assembly on the shaft and the bearing, before tapping the shaft again from the opposite end. A puller may be used to remove the bearing (Fig. 4.22)

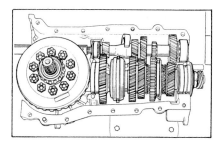

Above **Fig. 4.17. Longitudinally-split casing allows easy shaft removal on the Renault 18**

Above **Fig. 4.18. Staked nut also carrying the speedometer drive gear of the Renault 5**

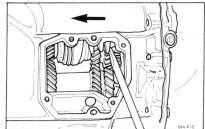

Above **Fig. 4.19. Selecting two gears simultaneously to lock gearbox shafts and prevent rotation**

Left **Fig. 4.20. Drifting roller bearing from web in the Renault 5 gearbox**

Fig. 4.21. The correct method of drifting shaft with a soft-faced mallet

Fig. 4.22. Using a universal puller to remove a roller bearing on a Peugeot 305

if there are suitable points to which to attach it, which is not always the case.

Laygear clusters in one-piece rear-wheel-drive gearboxes are slightly different in that they run on a plain shaft, usually with needle roller bearings between the plain shaft and the laygear. This type of layshaft is removed by undoing the inner shaft retainer and drifting the inner shaft from the casing with a small-diameter clean steel rod. This is usually carried out before removal of the mainshaft to

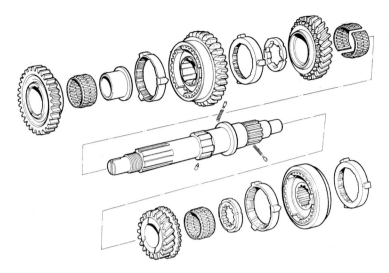

Fig. 4.23. Snap-fit retaining ring and plunger system (Mini and Leyland transverse mainshaft)

allow it clearance, the layshaft remaining in the bottom of the casing until the mainshaft has been removed.

With the shafts free from the casing they can be stripped to individual components. If any bearings remain at either end of the shafts, these should be removed with a suitable puller to allow the shaft components to be removed. The two principal shafts of the gearbox will usually be quite different, one carrying only the fixed gear wheels and the other carrying the free gears and synchronizer assemblies (the layshaft and mainshaft respectively in a rear-wheel-drive gearbox). In some cases both fixed and free gears are mixed on the shafts, in which case both shafts will require stripping, such as the Volkswagen Beetle in chapter 2. As ever when dismantling, it is of great help to keep all the components in order as they are removed and also in the correct orientation with respect to the shaft. Very often a retainer, or thrust washer, is very slightly asymmetrical and this can be very difficult to make out in an exploded diagram, which makes reassembly guesswork.

The gearbox shaft components are retained by three principal methods. External circlips are often used to retain components, as are interference or shrink-fit collars. Less often used is a snap-fit retaining ring with a plunger or plungers to locate it on the shaft. Some circlips used on gearbox shafts have conventional lugs and holes, while others, sometimes known as horseshoe circlips, have none and must be removed from the shaft using special flat-ended circlip pliers. If conventional circlip pliers are used it is worthwhile buying a good pair with properly tempered ends, as the larger circlips can easily slip and damage a bearing surface on the shaft. Snap-fit retaining rings (Fig. 4.23) can be tricky to remove, as several plungers may have to be lifted at the same time while the ring is rotated or removed. Enlisting help and finding just the right size and shape of jeweller's screwdriver or other implement to lift the plungers is a good idea.

Interference-fit collars are probably the most difficult fastening to deal with for the DIY mechanic. If there is enough of a lip on the collar it may be possible to remove it with a universal puller, but often there is insufficient purchase for the puller. Reference to the workshop manual may show that the collar can be removed if the shaft is heated and a kitchen oven can usually achieve the temperatures required. Handling the hot shaft afterwards and actually removing the collar can still be very difficult. If heating is not specified or unsuccessful, recourse can be made to a local engineering works, who will be used to this sort of problem and will be able to remove the collar with a press. Do not on any account grip the collar in a metal-jawed vice in an attempt to drift it from the shaft. Moderate impact may be used to try to remove a collar, but metal-faced hammers and vices will distort the collar and possibly damage the shaft. Use rubber- or plastic-faced vices and hammers.

Component inspection

When all the fastener problems have been surmounted, you will end up with a collection of bearings, gears and synchronizer components to be inspected (Fig. 4.24). To keep them in order they can be laid out in a line on a sheet of paper with all the sides facing towards one end of the shaft uppermost. In most cases it will not have been necessary to disassemble the synchronizer yet, so these can now be separated. Internal snap rings holding blocker bars should be removed carefully to prevent them distorting. If spring-loaded balls or plungers are used between the synchronizer

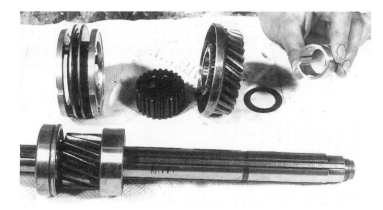

Fig. 4.24. Peugeot 305 gearbox components ready for inspection

hub and sleeve, the two parts should be separated with the synchronizer inside a large container to catch the ball or plungers as they fly out.

The types of bearing used on gearbox shafts include plain bushes, enclosed ball and taper roller bearings and needle roller bearings running directly on the shafts. When dismantling the bearings, the presence of dirt or grit should be noted, as any abrasive particles present must have been in the gearbox during operation and damage is therefore likely. Plain bushes should be free from scoring or pitting and have an even, dull, matt surface if they are wearing normally. Plain bushes are most often used for the free gears on the shafts and may be pressed into the gears or fixed to the shaft with the gear rotating on them. If fitted into the gear wheels, it may be possible to have them pressed out and new bushes fitted and reamed to the correct diameter. In other cases replacement bushes will not be available and a new gear wheel will have to be purchased. Bushes fixed to the shafts as in the Peugeot 204/304/305 gearbox (Fig. 4.25) are removable when the shaft is dismantled and easily replaced. If the bush is excessively worn the bearing surface of the gear wheel or shaft should also be examined closely, as this may have a burr or score, which will immediately damage the new bush.

Needle roller bearings running directly on the shaft and inside the gear wheel or layshaft are the most common form of bearing for these components. The shaft surfaces

Fig. 4.25. Plain bushes used on the Peugeot 305 output shaft

and insides of the gear wheels or layshaft must be completely free from pits or scores and indentations for these bearings to be reliable. If damage is found, the only remedy is to renew the components concerned. The needle rollers themselves are difficult to inspect visually over their whole surface, especially if caged as they usually are in modern gearboxes.

If any wear is apparent on the rollers or the shaft, the needle rollers should be replaced. While dealing with the rest of the gearbox the needle rollers are best kept separately and wrapped up to prevent abrasive contamination. If the rollers are accidentally dropped on to the floor or otherwise exposed to grit, they should be cleaned thoroughly before reassembly. With free rollers this simply means washing them in solvent, but caged rollers should be rotated rapidly in the solvent around a finger or shaft to flush out trapped grit. If the rollers do not rotate completely freely and smoothly after this, they should be replaced.

Conventional one-piece ball or taper roller bearings used to support shafts in gearboxes may be easily separable in some cases, but do not use great force. If a bearing is separable then the races and rollers can be inspected as described above for needle roller bearings. If not separable then the bearing must be tested for freedom of rotation and roughness in operation. If any roughness is detected while rotating the bearing and loading it in its normal direction, then the bearing should be replaced. Contamination can be removed from one-piece bearings as with caged needle rollers.

The gear wheels will usually only show excessive wear or damage if lumps of swarf or broken components have been circulating in the gearbox. Metal lumps can result from broken dog clutch teeth, broken gears or the breakdown of case hardening on the gearbox shafts. If no contamination has been present then the gear teeth should show either no discernible wear or an even wear pattern, if a high mileage has been covered. If damage is present due to swarf or metal chips, it is usually widespread and the gear wheels affected will have to be replaced. Sometimes, however, damage is restricted to the odd chipped tooth end on a couple of gears and it may be decided to tolerate this degree of damage, as it is unlikely to get worse.

Often going hand in hand with gear tooth damage is damage to the dog teeth on the gears and synchronizer assemblies. Clutch maladjustment or misuse results in chipped dog teeth and metal chippings, which then cause damage to the gear wheels. Slight burring of the dog teeth may be accepted but heavy chipping or completely sheared teeth mean that the gear or synchronizer sleeve affected should be replaced. Unfortunately some synchromesh designs are not effective enough to prevent gradual dog tooth damage and so eventual component replacement is necessary. Wear to synchronizer hubs and sleeves, other than to the dog teeth, is less common, but the likely areas of wear are the selector-fork contact face and the sliding between hub and sleeve. Again slight wear is acceptable, but scoring or chipping is not.

The synchromesh friction clutch surfaces (Fig. 4.26) are prone to wear, either slowly or rapidly, depending on the design. Wear of these surfaces, unless obvious visually, in which case the baulk ring or gear should be replaced, is best judged by using the clearance figure test described later in reassembly. Visible wear often takes the form of a pitted, rough surface on the gear-mounted cone.

Fig. 4.26. Synchronizer clutch surfaces in Getrag gearbox

The shafts themselves almost always show damage only on bearing surfaces. The shafts should be checked paying particular attention to the bearing surfaces, where any pitting or scoring will mean replacement, but also checking threaded portions for stripping and splines for burring or wear.

The last part to be inspected is the casing itself. The casing or sections of casing should be cleaned inside using paraffin or alcohol after any remaining bearings or other removable components have been taken out. A brush can be used to loosen any detritus from corners of the casing and all swarf, broken dog teeth, etc, should be removed. All the bearing bores should be checked for scoring or other signs of wear, as this can indicate that the roller bearing outer race is rotating in the bore. Slight looseness of the bearing in the bore can be remedied by using a bearing locking compound, such as Loctite, when reassembling the bearing into the case, but any great degree of wear will require the replacement of the casing. The casing should also be checked visually for cracks, if there is any reason to suspect that it is damaged, perhaps due to the car having been involved in a collision. Before commencing re-assembly the selector shaft bores and any other holes or cavities in the casing should also be cleaned with a bottle brush or other suitable brush and the cleaning fluid allowed to drain away thoroughly to prevent dilution of the gearbox oil.

Reassembly
Reassembly of the gearbox is invariably carried out in the reverse order of removal and is best accomplished with reference to the *specific* instructions. Extra operations must be carried out when reassembling, to ensure that the working tolerances of the internal components are kept within the manufacturer's specified limits.

The tolerances relate to running clearances, bearing preloads and endfloats and to general distancing of components. Some boxes require far less checking and adjustment in these respects than others, although virtually all will require that taper and ball-race bearings are given the correct amount of preload (elimination of play by clamping action), while thrust washers and gear wheels are allowed the correct amount of endfloat (free side-play) to ensure friction-free rotation without excessive lateral movement.

Another frequent adjustment is to the distance between gear wheels and synchronizer hubs (to ensure synchromesh efficiency), and this goes hand in hand with gear wheel endfloat adjustment, as it is determined by the latter. Not all mainshaft designs incorporate this adjustment though, and excessive synchro distances or gear wheel endfloats can only be corrected by expensive component renewal.

The first components to be reassembled are usually the synchronizer units which, with the exception of the Peugeot/Buick one-piece type, comprise a central hub, an outer sleeve, often two snap rings or three coil springs and balls, and blocker bars/slippers (where fitted). Some

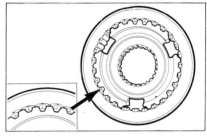

Left **Fig. 4.27. This is a Getrag synchronizer assembly shown disassembled**

Above **Fig. 4.28. Triumph Acclaim (Honda) synchronizer has a larger (master) spline to ensure correct hub-to-sleeve alignment**

designs of synchronizer have no detent springs but rely solely on the action of the selector detents. The Getrag synchronizer, shown disassembled in Fig. 4.27, has no integral detents.

When sliding the sleeve over the central hub, check the manufacturer's directions: there may be a master spline to determine a certain correct angular relationship between the two (Fig. 4.28), or else an alignment marking. On synchros using coil spring and ball-type detents it is necessary to compress the three detents at the same time in order to allow the sleeve to pass over them. This is most easily achieved using a piston ring compressor or purpose-built conical compressing ring and applying the same technique as for fitting pistons to cylinder bores. ALWAYS carry out this operation inside a bag, as if your compressing ring slips and a detent ball is fired off by its spring you will probably never see it again! When the unit is assembled, click the sleeve back and forth by hand to make sure that it is moving freely and detenting into its 'gear engaged' positions.

On synchronizer types using internal snap rings for the detents (Fig. 4.29) the assembly operation is far less stressful; make sure, however, that the snap rings engage in the groove in each blocker bar/slipper (where applicable) and that the curved ends of the rings lie in the positions stipulated by the manufacturer (Fig. 4.30).

Invariably the next step is the reassembly of the mainshaft, as this comprises the greatest number of individual items but is installed to the gearbox housing as one piece. The different fastening devices used on

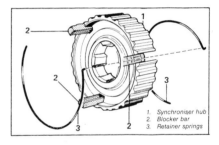

1. Synchroniser hub
2. Blocker bar
3. Retainer springs

Above **Fig. 4.29. This design of synchronizer uses internal spring rings to detent sleeve positions**

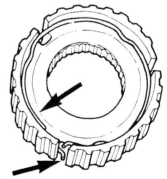

Above **Fig. 4.30. Many synchronizer spring rings have only one raised end and must be fitted opposing one another**

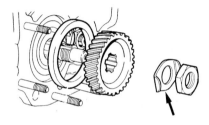

Above **Fig. 4.31. The tab washer (arrowed) prevents the nut on this Leyland mainshaft from undoing itself. The gear shown is the bottom transfer gear, driven by the idler gear**

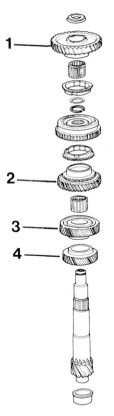

Fig. 4.32. Exploded view of a VW Polo input shaft—free first (4) and second (3) gears plus locking third (1) and fourth (2) gears are mixed

mainshaft assemblies have already been listed and rarely need renewing, although any circlip (whatever type of circlip) that has been bent or in any way distorted upon removal *must* be replaced with a new one. Where a nut or bolt is used as a mainshaft fastening device and is prevented from accidental loosening by a *tab washer* (Fig. 4.31), the tab washer should not be reused unless it is designed with more than one edge or face that can be turned up. A deformable locking device such as this fatigues when bent and so cannot be trusted to do its job reliably a second time. Some retaining nuts used on gearbox shafts are fitted with a staking collar which should be deformed on to a flat, or into a recess, at the end of the shaft. These nuts should always be renewed.

Some screw-threaded fastening devices are prevented from accidental loosening by the application of thread sealing compound such as Loctite so always check whether this is required. The snap-fit retaining ring and plunger method of mainshaft component retention (Fig. 4.23), as used on the Leyland 'gears-in-sump' gearbox, is tricky to deal with and often requires three hands and more fingers than you've got; it pays to make sure there's someone around to help you with it when the time comes to refit it, and also to fit it while working with mainshaft and hands inside a plastic bag to avoid losing the plunger or spring(s).

The DIY man's 'favourite' enemy, the interference-fit component, can often cause DIY activity to take an enforced break while the professionals take over. Heating a component such as a plain steel bearing or a speedometer drive gear to the correct temperature for it to expand sufficiently to be fitted over the shaft, is not necessarily as easy as it sounds, while finding a hammer-and-drift alternative to the gently applied 3-or-more tons' pressure of a hydraulic press can result in frustration and damaged components.

On some cars such as the VW Beetle, Polo and Golf, a slightly unconventional design of gearbox is used, where mainshaft and countershaft (layshaft) functions are mixed, each shaft (now referred to as input and output shafts) bearing one synchronizer unit for a pair of gears (Fig. 4.32). With such a design it is common practice for some of the gear wheels to be shrink-fitted to the shafts (interference-fitting by heating one component so that it expands, fitting it on to another and letting it cool down and shrink while doing so). This requires them to be heated to more than 100 degrees Celsius and pressed on with suitable equipment.

Shrink-fit components can be heated by submersion in hot oil, laying on a hotplate, or 'baking' in an oven, but in each case their temperature must be assessed. The temperature of a hot oil bath can be verified with a suitably calibrated thermometer (and we hasten to add, *great* care must be exercised when dealing with a container full of scalding oil) while hotplate and oven methods require a different technique for verification of the component's temperature. Some manufacturers specify that certain components have reached the desired temperature for fitting when a piece of solder melts on them, while others are more exacting and suggest that you mark the items in question with a *thermochromatic pencil*, the markings from which will change colour when a certain temperature is reached. Thermochromatic pencils are available for different heat ranges.

Our advice on the matter of assembling interference-fit components is quite simple: if the item can be tapped into position with judicious use of a hammer and drift, then that's fine. If you know the temperature to which the item must be heated and you have a safe method of heating it and can check the temperature, then all's well and good. Frustrated belting with a big mallet, however, will ultimately result in far more expense and inconvenience than a trip down to your local engineering works with the mainshaft components in a box!

We do not aim to be specific in detailing how to reassemble a mainshaft and it would in fact be quite impossible to give specific information in view of the many different executions that exist. For assembly procedures therefore, you must refer to the relevant workshop manual. We would advise, however, that you take time to read the following tips before commencing reassembly:

1) For the sake of the bearings and bearing surfaces, make sure that your hands are clean and grit-free. For the same

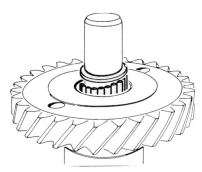

Above **Fig. 4.33. With uncaged needle rollers, make sure you have** *exactly* **the correct number**

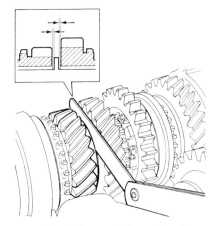

Above **Fig. 4.34. Measuring the endfloat of a mainshaft gear wheel**

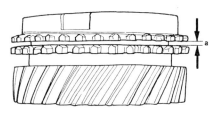

Above **Fig. 4.35. The remaining clearance between gear wheel dog teeth and baulk ring edge indicates the degree of wear**

reason, don't work on any surface other than a clean one and have an abundant supply of new rags with which to wipe any grit or 'gungy' oil off the mainshaft components.

2) It is essential to lubricate every moving part with oil as you assemble, so use fresh oil (the grade normally specified for your particular transmission unit) as you assemble and be lavish in its application.

3) If an uncaged needle roller bearing is used on a shaft (Fig. 4.33)—and these are often found in the layshaft cluster—which comprises only a set of thin steel needles, make sure that you have *exactly* the number of needles specified in the manual. DON'T be tempted to make do with 20 needles where there should be 21—this is courting disaster. Loose needle roller bearings are best fitted into place (whether on to the shaft or into the bore of a gear wheel) by sticking them together and to their location with multi-purpose grease. Don't worry about any adverse effects that the grease might have when the gearbox is in use . . . it won't, as it will soon dissolve into the oil.

4) All components that are designed to spin freely on the mainshaft (i.e. the gear wheels) have to have a certain amount of *endfloat*—the minimal amount by which the gear wheels can slide back and forth along the shaft. If there were no clearance between the gear wheels and their *thrust washers* (the bearings at their sides which restrict sideways movement) then they would not spin freely. However, if too much endfloat is allowed then not only is excessive noise generated and pinion 'chatter' too, but the critical distance between the gear wheel and the synchronizer is upset, thereby causing inefficient gear-change synchronization. Workshop manuals nearly always specify an endfloat, to be measured by feeler gauge between the gear and its thrust stop, as shown in Fig. 4.34, though not all gearboxes provide for adjustment of the endfloat if it is excessive due to wear.

Adjustment is usually effected by choosing shims or spacers of selective thickness with which to 'pack out' the mainshaft components in order to reduce gear endfloats to the desired figure (Fig. 4.36). Where adjustment is not provided, but wear is none the less excessive, a cure can only be effected by replacing the thrust stop/washer (if it's

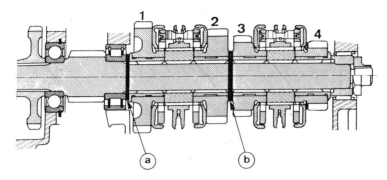

Fig. 4.36. This Peugeot mainshaft assembly uses variable-thickness shims to determine gear wheel endfloat

removable) or the shaft (if it's not), or the gear wheel(s) in question until an endfloat is obtained that is within specified tolerances. We have rebuilt gearboxes in which we were forced to allow excessive (according to specification) endfloats on gear wheels due to financial limitations. In our experience of doing this we have found it rare that a gear wheel endfloat is so critical that it will cause operational problems, and sometimes it is expedient to 'stretch' this tolerance a little where it would not be justifiable to buy new components. For instance, an endfloat of 0.017 in. on a gear wheel which has a specified maximum of 0.011 in. has been run reliably and satisfactorily in a gearbox before now.

The most likely detrimental effects of excessive gear endfloat are increased lever travel and poor synchronization of that gear, but this has not been found to be a problem with only slightly too great an endfloat. This brings us on to the next 'adjustable' settings to be looked out for when tackling mainshaft reassembly.

5) For a baulk ring to grip a gear wheel cone 100 per cent effectively, it must be able to ride up that cone and form a perfect taper-fit on it without contacting the edge of the gear's dog-tooth ring. If the cone or the inside surface of the baulk ring (Fig. 4.26) is worn down, the ring will have to travel further up the cone before gripping it fully, and the clearance left between the edge of the dog-tooth ring and the baulk ring when cone and ring are pushed together hard (Fig. 4.35) will be an accurate reflection of the amount by which the cone clutch is worn. The gearbox manufacturer will specify an acceptable range of clearances

Fig. 4.37. Measuring synchro cone wear

Fig. 4.38 The Peugeot/Buick synchronizer assembly

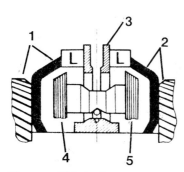

Fig. 4.39. This is the Peugeot/Buick-type synchronizer in simplified section; the blocks 'L' represent fixed-width blocks which check the clearance between the female cone and the synchro control sleeve (1—gear/synchro cone 1; 2—gear synchro cone 2; 3—synchro control sleeve; 4—synchro male cone 1; 5—synchro male cone 2)

(again, to be measured with a feeler gauge as in Fig. 4.37) and if too small a clearance is obtained then a new baulk ring should be purchased (these tend to be quite cheap) and the measurement procedure repeated with it. If the clearance remains too small then this is indicative of wear of the synchronizer cone, necessitating renewal of the gear wheel in question. It isn't necessary for either the gear wheel or the baulk ring to be fitted to the mainshaft for the purpose of this wear check and it is best to carry the check out with *dry* cone clutch surfaces.

Insufficient cone clutch grip results in poor synchronization and gear clash, and, where this has been occurring, there is usually tell-tale damage to the dog teeth of that gear, such as heavy burring of the tooth bevels or chipped and sometimes *missing* teeth. Incidentally, if a gear wheel needs replacing, it is not always necessary to replace its corresponding gear wheel on the opposite shaft, although there is a slight risk that the new gear will generate some noise when transmitting torque to its corresponding, partly-worn gear. The higher the mileage already accomplished by the gears, the greater the risk of this noise being generated, as the difference in tooth forms between old and new wheels will not be conducive to perfect meshing.

6) The Peugeot/Buick-type synchronizer (Fig. 4.38), having no separate baulk ring, is checked for wear when the mainshaft is reassembled and *in situ* in the gearbox housing. Referring to Fig. 4.39 it can be seen that by introducing a fixed-width gauge (L) between each gear wheel cone and the synchronizer control sleeve, it can be assessed whether the distance between the synchronizer (and thus the male part of the cone clutch) and the gear cone is too great or too little; ideally the gauge should be a tight push-fit. Adjustment of this measurement can then be effected by selective differential shimming of the gear wheels on either side of the synchronizer as shown at A and B in Fig. 4.36.

7) With the mainshaft assembled, the next step in rebuilding is preparation of the housing to accept its internal components. The housing will have at least one gasket face, and usually more, depending on the design,

and all of these faces must be carefully cleaned to ensure effective oil sealing when new gaskets are fitted. When scraping old gasket material and sealing compound off iron casings it is all right to use a metal tool such as a knife, or better still, a Stanley knife-type blade. Handles can be cheaply obtained for these blades which allow them to be used as scrapers. It is not advisable to use metal implements to scrape the mating faces of an aluminium alloy housing though, unless absolutely necessary, as the soft aluminium is very easily gouged and a less than smooth sealing surface may well cause oil leaks later on. In practice it may be very difficult to scrape hardened gasket material off such surfaces using anything softer than a metal scraper. If you are confronted with stubborn gasket material then use a blade to shift it, but be *very* careful not to cut into the metal and be prepared to spend a long time doing it.

A quick and easy way to aid removal of stubborn gasket material is to brush it liberally with paint stripper, wait a few minutes and then scrape it off—this avoids the need for any forceful use of the scraper and so less damage is likely to be caused. A good tip for removing old, hardened gasket jointing compound, such as Hammerite, is to dissolve it with methylated spirit. Silicone rubber 'gasket substitute' is usually easy to peel off by hand in long strips as it has the consistency of rubber and so binds together.

Before fitting any components to the gearbox housing, probe all bolt and stud holes with a piece of wire to ensure that there is no dirt caught in them. Gearbox housings very often have a magnetic *swarf collector* located at some point, usually towards the bottom; it is often removable, especially when combined with the drain plug (if fitted) but can also be fixed permanently to the housing. In either case, wipe all metal particles off the magnet. Fig. 4.40 shows a swarf collector being removed from the front-wheel-drive Ford Escort gearbox.

8) With the mainshaft assembly installed in the housing, it is nearly always necessary to check and adjust the *preload* of its support bearings. Some modern gearboxes, however, by virtue of their exact manufacturing tolerances and bearing design, have shafts which run without preload and

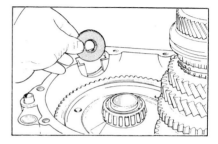

Fig. 4.40. The fwd Ford Escort's magnetic swarf collector

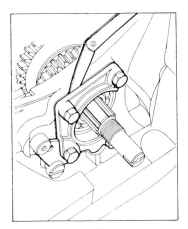

Above **Fig. 4.41. Mini mainshaft has bearing retainer plate; gap behind it is being measured with feeler gauges to determine required preload shims**

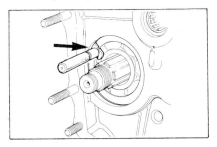

Above **Fig. 4.42. Mini gearbox output shaft; end bearing circlip groove is being measured to determine required thickness of bearing circlip**

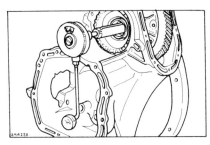

Above **Fig. 4.43. Torque gauge checking Astra differential**

so do not require any setting-up: the Vauxhall Nova/Astra/Cavalier unit is one example

Preload, as mentioned previously, is the amount of clamping or 'nip' to which a ball-race or taper roller bearing is subjected. This 'nip' is achieved by pulling the shaft and bearing inner tracks together against the outer tracks, thereby 'squeezing' the balls or rollers. This can be effected by packing or *shimming* behind a bearing retainer plate (Fig. 4.41), by locating one of the end bearings with a circlip of carefully selected thickness (Fig. 4.42), or by measuring the amount of torque it takes to turn the shaft with the bearings clamped. This last method is the rarest and requires the use of a special torque gauge (like the one shown checking the turning torque of a Vauxhall Astra differential in Fig. 4.43).

Endfloat is easy to measure by means of either feeler gauges or a dial gauge (Fig. 4.44) but, because preload is a compression, it is not directly measurable and has to be calculated. Often this is carried out by setting a certain, measured amount of endfloat and then adding shims or selecting a circlip of sufficient thickness to eliminate that endfloat as well as introducing the required preload, measured in millimetres. As an example, a mainshaft bearing, specified to have 0.1 mm preload (by shim), when installed without any shims registers an endfloat of 0.3 mm. Therefore a shim or shims of 0.4 mm total thickness should be employed.

The layshaft often runs with endfloat, especially when it is supported on needle roller bearings; in this situation it invariably has a thrust washer at either end, to take the axial thrust generated by the helical teeth and to determine the endfloat (Fig. 4.45). Usually only one washer is available in different thicknesses. An alternative arrangement is where the layshaft gear cluster is mounted on taper roller or angular contact ball-race bearings at either end, both of which bearing types take the thrust loadings generated by the shaft and require preloading (Fig. 4.46).

9) A layshaft gear cluster which runs on a separate shaft, and has internal uncaged needle rollers, requires the use of a second similar shaft when reassembling to the housing. This is because the needle rollers are unlikely to stay in

position inside the cluster (even when greased) if a shaft is not present. The original shaft has to be removed from the housing to allow the laygear cluster to be lifted out in the first place, but obviously cannot be lowered back in with the cluster as it is longer than the distance between the housing supports. Thus a shaft of the same diameter but the same length as the laygear must be kept inside the cluster when the latter is positioned in the gearbox. Once in place and aligned with the housing bores, the layshaft can be tapped in through the casing, thus driving out the dummy shaft. It is important that both shafts are kept in contact throughout this procedure. Clearly the ideal dummy shaft to use for this operation is an old layshaft which has been cut down to the appropriate length. To locate the thrust washers before installing the laygear cluster, first stick them to the edge of each housing bore with grease (Fig. 4.47).

10) There is little to be said of a general nature about the installation of selector rails, rods, forks, detents and interlock devices, other than to ensure that you fit them in the casing at the correct stage of assembly (a different stage in each type of box). It is quite easy to omit one or more detent balls, plungers or springs when reassembling, as there are so many of them in certain designs of gearbox; it pays to have a careful count-up of these before fitting them.

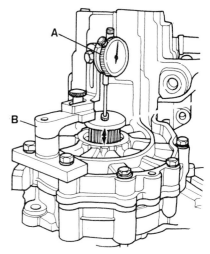

Above **Fig. 4.44.** Measuring the final drive endfloat of a VW Golf gearbox, using a dial gauge and mounting bracket

Top left **Fig. 4.45.** Conventional layshaft/laygear assembly which uses needle roller bearings and thrust washers (1—layshaft; 2—thrust washer; 3—needle bearing assembly; 4—laygear cluster)

Below left **Fig. 4.46.** This layshaft/laygear assembly employs angular contact bearings (1—angular contact ball-race bearings; 2—layshaft)

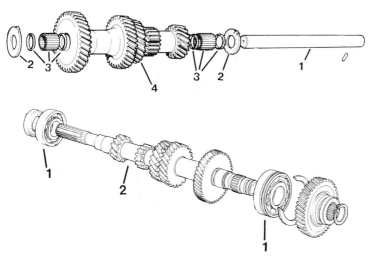

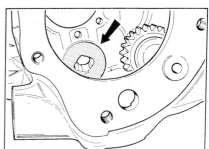

Above **Fig. 4.47.** Sierra gearbox has its layshaft thrust washers stuck in place with grease prior to layshaft/laygear assembly

Also make sure that detent springs of different rates (not always noticeable at first sight) go into their correct locations. Fig. 4.48 shows the detents and selectors from a Renault 5 transaxle; the middle spring is much longer than the others but this is not apparent *in situ*.

11) Sealing of the housing is usually one of the final stages, and may include oil seal, O-ring and gasket fitment, the application of jointing compound, and thread sealing of certain bolts and set screws.

The section at the beginning of this chapter, detailing working methods, gives hints on oil seal replacement. O-rings are usually found where a pressurized oil supply passes from one casting to another, or if the gearbox itself acts as the engine's oil sump pan; in this case a strainer will be fitted in the bottom of the housing, often connected to a pick-up pipe or passageway with an O-ring seal (arrowed, Fig. 4.49). O-rings should not be reused if they are soft and flabby, brittle or compressed.

Fig. 4.48. The Renault 5's selector detent springs; the middle one is much longer than the others but this is not apparent when the springs are *in situ*

Fig. 4.49. This Peugeot 305 'gears-in-sump' gearbox has an oil pick-up strainer which filters oil drawn from the bottom of the gearbox. It connects to the pick-up hole and this joint is sealed by an O-ring

Paper gaskets are best fitted with a jointing compound such as Red Hermetite, spread evenly over both mating surfaces, even if the manufacturer does not mention its application. Not only does the compound help hold the gaskets in position before the casings are joined, but it guarantees effective oil tightness, even of slightly damaged faces.

Bolts or set screws which communicate between the inside of the gearbox housing and the outside, must have a thread sealing compound applied to ensure that oil cannot work its way up the thread and leak out. When tightening the retaining bolts or nuts of an aluminium or pressed steel casting or cover, never exceed the specified torque and tighten them in a progressive order, to avoid causing distortion. Some gearboxes have a specific nut/bolt tightening sequence specified; Fig. 4.7 (on page 71) shows the complicated tightening sequence for the casings of a Renault 18 transaxle.

Chapter 5 | Final drives and differentials

Final drives

The term 'final drive' is conventionally applied to the last stage in the transmission of power from the engine to the road wheels, excluding the differential. It can be difficult to determine what the final drive components of some more unusual cars, such as DAFs, actually are, but in the majority of cars covered by this book the term is applied to the pair of gears driving the differential. The type of gears used for the purpose depends on the transmission layout. Spur gears (Fig. 5.1) are used where the power is transmitted between parallel shafts, such as in transverse-engined cars, and bevel gears where the drive is between shafts at right-angles, such as in inline-engined cars. The worm-and-wheel type of gearing (Fig. 5.2) has also been used in cars, most notably Peugeot 404s, but this is uncommon and will not be covered in this chapter.

The gears used in final drives are universally helical gears in order to reduce the noise generated, as the final drive gears carry the highest torque loading of all the gears in the transmission. Only one arrangement exists in spur-gear final drives, but in bevel-gear final drives both ordinary helical bevel (Fig. 5.3) and 'hypoid' bevel (Fig. 5.4) gears are used. Ordinary helical bevel gears require that the driving gear be placed at the centre height of the driven gear, i.e. the driving gear axis must intersect the differential axis. Hypoid gears allow the driving gear to be placed below (or above) the differential axis, allowing the propshaft to intrude less into the floorpan of rear-wheel-drive cars than with helical bevel gears. This type of gear was developed specifically for automobile applications because of this feature. Hypoid gears have the disadvan-

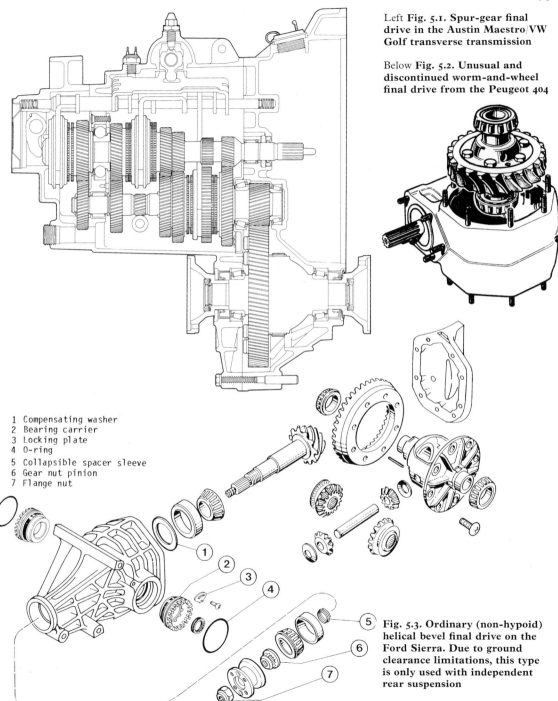

Left **Fig. 5.1. Spur-gear final drive in the Austin Maestro/VW Golf transverse transmission**

Below **Fig. 5.2. Unusual and discontinued worm-and-wheel final drive from the Peugeot 404**

1 Compensating washer
2 Bearing carrier
3 Locking plate
4 O-ring
5 Collapsible spacer sleeve
6 Gear nut pinion
7 Flange nut

Fig. 5.3. Ordinary (non-hypoid) helical bevel final drive on the Ford Sierra. Due to ground clearance limitations, this type is only used with independent rear suspension

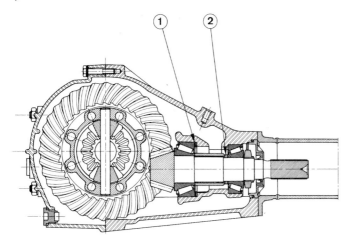

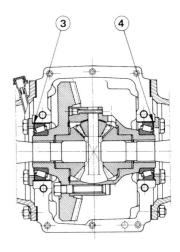

Fig. 5.4. Hypoid bevel final drive of the Peugeot 404, showing clearly the offset pinion

tage, as a consequence, of creating a sliding contact between the gear teeth, which makes them more susceptible to failure and necessitates the use of special hypoid lubricants. Adjustment of hypoid gears is also more critical.

Disassembly

The disassembly of any type of final drive will almost always require the removal of the final drive/differential casing from the car. It may be tempting to try to carry out an overhaul with the unit still in the car, but more often than not this causes problems at a later stage and therefore we recommend its removal. In a rear-wheel-drive car this will entail the removal of the live axle, or the differential housing in the case of independent suspension. With a transverse front- (or rear-) wheel-drive layout the final drive/differential is usually housed in the gearbox casing, which may be removable separately from the engine or may require the removal of the whole power unit to separate the gearbox.

Chapter 4 covers disassembly of gearbox casings and applies equally to final drive casings. When access has been gained to the final drive/differential assembly the differential may be removed to allow inspection on the workbench. The bearings supporting the differential are in most cases removed with the differential and the caps or adjusters retaining them should be released. Make a note of any shims present, if a cap or flange is used, or mark a threaded adjuster and count the number of turns it unscrews. This will allow the differential to be replaced with the same bearing adjustments, which are likely to be correct or nearly correct. The final drive pinion may also be removed, but, if on an inline-engined rear-wheel-drive car it is easily inspected without its removal and no wear is apparent in the bearings supporting it, it is possible that time may be saved setting the pinion mesh later if it is left in place, as the mesh may then be right (though this must be checked).

Inspection

As mentioned in the previous section, the final drive gears carry the highest loading of any gears in the transmission and so are reasonably likely to show wear, especially if maintenance has been neglected. Spur-gear final drives are the least likely to wear and in practice rarely give trouble unless mistreated. Hypoid and plain bevel final drive gears will almost certainly show some marking on the surface if the vehicle has covered any mileage. Inspection must be carried out to determine whether the wear level is acceptable. No hard and fast rule can easily be given to dictate when wear is excessive as this depends on the usage and required life of the gearset.

An enthusiast with a small-engined classic car covering a low annual mileage can afford to accept a greater degree of wear than would be acceptable on a powerful car used every day, so the following should be treated as guidelines, depending on the vehicle. The same amount of wear should be considered more serious on highly loaded hypoid gears and relatively less serious on plain bevel and spur gears. Pitting or scoring of the gear contact surfaces means that the gears should be renewed, unless only a few pits or indentations exist on a few teeth of the gears and it appears that this is not causing an acceleration of the existing wear or damage. Similarly, chips taken out of the gears indicate the need for renewal unless only very few and minor chips exist and these are not on the load-bearing areas of the teeth. Polishing of the gear contact surfaces is normal, as may be a slight discolouration of the surface due to dirty oil. Abnormal wear of the teeth without pitting or scoring is harder to detect, but may be shown up by looking at the teeth end-on. Any visible asymmetry of the tooth profile indicates serious wear.

The final drive bearings should also be inspected for wear as bearing wear causes accelerated gear wear and bearing failure is serious in itself. The bearings should be completely free to rotate and should be free from catches or roughness when loaded in their usual directions and rotated. Bearings are readily available and much less expensive than gears and so should be replaced at any sign of wear.

Reassembly and adjustment
Spur-gear final drives usually have the correct gear mesh set during manufacture, as it is dictated by the centre spacing of the pinion support bearing and the differential bearings. If there is a problem with the final drive gears in such an arrangement then check the differential bearings and the differential run-out (side-play) as this is likely to be the source of the problem. If the mesh is still not satisfactory (check as described later) with correct differential bearing adjustments then the between-centre distance of the gears should be checked. This will require a manufacturer's special distance jig or precision measuring table and gauges and is not within the scope of most home mechanics. A manufacturer's agent should have the gauge required and will carry out the work for a small charge, if presented with the bare casing and final drive gears. If the distance is found to be incorrect the only solution is to renew the casing carrying the final drive gears. If mesh adjustment is possible then proceed as described below for bevel gears (except, of course, leaving out the pinion distance adjustment). Preloading of the pinion support bearing should not be required.

With helical and hypoid bevel final drives the adjustment of mesh and bearing preload is much more critical. These types of gear, if incorrectly meshed, can wear rapidly without producing much noise and then fail (very noisily).

The preload of the pinion bearings is set either by a preload torque setting, shims or by a collapsible spacer (Fig. 5.5), which concertinas at the required preload. The correct preload method for your car should be found in the workshop manual and followed closely. Whichever method is employed, the desired result is to achieve absolutely NO PLAY in the pinion support bearings. If play still exists then the preload is incorrect.

The differential support bearings are adjusted either by threaded adjusters (Fig. 5.6) or by shims. If shims are used the preload procedure consists of adding too great a thickness of shims under the bearing flange, nipping the flange down lightly on to the shims and then measuring the gap between flange and housing with feeler gauges. The excess thickness of shim is then removed, less a prescribed 'pinch' distance to preload the bearing. Where threaded adjusters are used and also sometimes with shims, the correct adjustment may be obtained by measuring the run-out of the differential gear. This is carried out by mounting a dial test indicator (DTI) on the differential housing and measuring the variation in reading as the differential is rotated and loaded in different directions with the DTI probe against its side (Fig. 5.7). The adjusters are then rotated, or shims added or removed, to achieve the required runout figure. This figure is very small and usually in the order of 0.05 mm. When setting the final drive gear mesh these preloads must be maintained or the correct mesh will not be obtained.

Setting the final drive gear mesh requires two separate adjustments. The first is the pinion distance, which is the distance of the pinion from the differential centre line. The other is the differential lateral adjustment, the correct centring of the differential between its support bearings. Both of these adjustments must be correct to achieve the correct mesh and good gear life. Manufacturers sometimes specify measurements between, for example, the pinion end face and the differential centre line, but these are difficult to measure correctly for the home mechanic and so the method described below is recommended. Some manufacturers stamp the pinion during assembly with a code indicating the correct thickness of shim to use to set

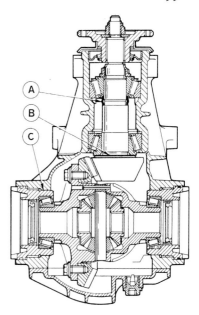

Fig. 5.5. Collapsible preload spacer, labelled 'A', in the Ford Sierra final drive

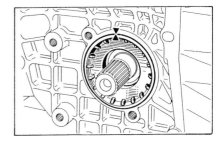

Fig. 5.6. Differential bearing adjuster ring nuts of the Renault 18. A locking plate engages with the splines to prevent rotation (not shown)

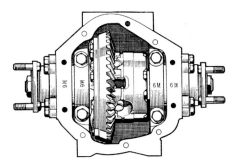

Above **Fig. 5.7. Differential bearing cap markings**

Right **Fig. 5.8. Tooth contact indication**

2883	TOOTH CONTACT (DRIVE GEAR)	CONDITION	REMEDY
A	HEEL (outer end), Coast, TOE (inner end), Drive	IDEAL TOOTH CONTACT Evenly spread over profile, nearer toe than heel.	o —— o
B	HEEL (outer end), f, Coast, TOE (inner end), Drive	HIGH TOOTH CONTACT Heavy on the top of the drive gear tooth profile.	Move the DRIVE PINION DEEPER INTO MESH. i.e., REDUCE the pinion cone setting.
C	HEEL (outer end), Coast, TOE (inner end), Drive	LOW TOOTH CONTACT Heavy in the root of the drive gear tooth profile.	Move the DRIVE PINION OUT OF MESH. i.e., INCREASE the pinion cone setting.
D	HEEL (outer end), Coast, TOE (inner end), Drive	TOE CONTACT Hard on the small end of the drive gear tooth.	Move the DRIVE GEAR OUT OF MESH. i.e., INCREASE backlash.
E	HEEL (outer end), Coast, TOE (inner end), Drive	HEEL CONTACT Hard on the large end of the drive gear tooth.	Move the DRIVE GEAR INTO MESH. i.e., DECREASE backlash but maintain minimum backlash as given in "Data"

the pinion protrusion distance. If you have access to a manufacturer's manual the code can be used to look up the correct shim thickness, but this will usually be the same as the thickness of shims removed, and with a higher mileage differential it is best to check the mesh as described below in any case.

The correctness of mesh of any gears can be determined by the parts of the gear tooth flanks in contact with each other during normal operation. This, of course, is not normally visible so the gears must be coated with something to indicate the areas of contact. Engineers' blue diluted with oil can be used for this as can a mixture of a dark paint and oil painted sparingly on to the gear teeth. The different errors of mesh are shown in Fig. 5.8. The cause of the error is labelled next to each pattern and should be remedied by changing shims or rotating the adjusters to move the gears in the directions indicated in the table. Correct mesh is indicated by the top pattern. This method will always work as long as the bearing preloads are correct, but it may take some patience to achieve recognizable patterns on the teeth.

Do not replace the differential until you are absolutely sure that the mesh is correct. Incorrect mesh can cause very rapid wear and failure and, as mentioned before, may not be accompanied by a noise until the damage has been done.

Differentials

The operation of the bevel gear differential has been described in chapter 1 and though other methods of achieving the same action exist, the bevel gear differential (Fig. 5.9) is used universally in automobile axles, as it is by far the simplest and most rugged design. A variation on the basic bevel gear differential is the friction-plate limited slip differential (LSD) (Fig. 5.10). This design of LSD has spring-preloaded friction plates between the sun wheels and the casing which limit the differential rotation of the output shafts. The clamping force from the springs is supplemented by the side thrust of the sun gears, providing a progressive locking of the differential as the applied torque is increased. In the case of the Thornton 'Powr-lok' differential illustrated, the four planet gears are mounted in pairs on cross shafts, which move outwards up ramps in the outer casing under torque, applying pressure to the sun wheels and the friction plates. The springs in this

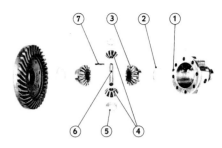

Above **Fig. 5.9. Peugeot 404: (1) differential body; (2) sun wheel thrust washer; (3) sun wheel; (4) planet wheels; (5) planet wheel thrust washers; (6) planet pin; (7) planet pin retainer**

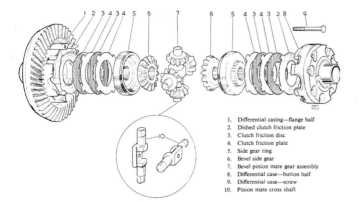

1. Differential casing—flange half
2. Dished clutch friction plate
3. Clutch friction disc
4. Clutch friction plate
5. Side gear ring
6. Bevel side gear
7. Bevel pinion mate gear assembly
8. Differential case—button half
9. Differential case—screw
10. Pinion mate cross shaft

Fig. 5.10. Thorton Powr-lok differential

design are the outer friction plates, which are dished to form a diaphragm spring, similar to a diaphragm clutch spring.

LSDs are used to improve the traction in slippery conditions and when cornering, but the commonly applied friction plate design also increases steering effort, even under low acceleration, due to the non-torque-dependent clamping springs. For this reason friction-plate LSDs have only been applied to high-performance cars, where steering effort is less important. This limitation has been removed by the 'viscous' LSD first used by Ferguson in the Jensen FF and used in the past few years in mass-production cars. This design limits the differential action with multiple counter-rotating plates immersed in a viscous oil. The torque required to rotate the plates past each other is proportional to their relative speed so that in normal low-speed manoeuvring the effect is negligible. If a wheel is spinning, however, the relative speed of the plates is high and a much larger locking torque is produced. In addition to the normal viscous effects of ordinary oils, special oils may be used which increase in viscosity when heated and so further increase the locking action if much wheel slip occurs. Because of the greater difficulty of overhauling the viscous-type LSD, you are advised to have a unit of this type serviced by a specialist.

Disassembly

In order to inspect the differential components of ordinary and friction-plate limited slip differentials it is necessary to separate the two halves of the differential body. These are normally held together by bolts around the edge of the body, which should be accessible without removing the differential support bearings. In some instances, such as for bearing renewal, their removal is required and a puller should be used in preference to levers or drifting the bearing off (Fig. 5.11). If an LSD is being dismantled the retaining bolts should be loosened progressively to release the spring pressure. When the two halves are separate the planet wheel cross shaft(s) may be drifted out to free the planet wheels and remaining sun wheel. These are commonly an interference-fit in the casing or may have a roll pin holding them. With a Thornton LSD the cross shafts are freed merely by separating the two halves of the differential body.

Inspection

Inspection of components is the same for ordinary and friction-plate limited slip differentials with the exception of the additional clutch components in the latter. In the experience of the authors, a greater degree of wear can be accepted in the differential gears than in other transmission gears, because of their comparatively low rotational speed and the fact that they are not permanently rotating. Replacement of the gears and cross shaft should be contemplated if the shaft is heavily worn or if the differential makes excessive noise when cornering. Wear of the gear teeth may be noticeable on higher mileage cars, but unless this amounts to serious erosion of the profile or breaking of the tooth surface, the gears could be reused by an economy-minded motorist.

If, of course, the components are readily and cheaply available, there is nothing preventing their replacement. Wear to the gear thrust washers is common and these are worth replacing if slightly worn, as they are comparatively cheap. If the differential wear is very severe or the casing is damaged, a cheaper alternative to replacing all the components may be the purchase of an exchange reconditioned unit. Be careful, however, to ensure that the unit has been rebuilt by a reputable company, as a back-street reconditioned unit may not be reliable

The clutch components in a friction-plate LSD should be free from major scoring. The amount of wear of the clutch surfaces can be judged by the wear ridge between the friction surface and the locating drive tangs on the outer edge. If a large ridge exists then it is likely that the action of the clutch is being impaired and the plates will need replacing. This can be evaluated more accurately by carrying out a slipping torque test with the differential reassembled, as described later.

Reassembly and adjustment

Reassembly of the differential is simply the reverse of the

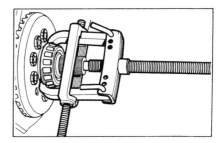

Fig. 5.11. Removing a differential bearing with a universal puller

disassembly procedure, as the differential gears usually require no shim adjustment. Should this be required, the procedure in the manufacturer's manual should be followed. Lock tabs on the bolts securing the differential halves should be replaced as a matter of course. With an LSD the bolts should be tightened progressively, as during disassembly

Some LSDs have an adjustment procedure involving measuring the torque required to rotate the output shafts relative to the differential body. This allows the effect of clutch plate wear to be measured and also shows up any weakening of the preload springs. The differential body should be firmly supported and a method found of attaching a torque wrench to the output shaft. The setting of the torque wrench should be set initially higher than the specified slipping torque and gradually reduced until the torque wrench 'breaks' just as the output shaft turns. If the torque figure is substantially less than dictated, then the clutch plates or preload springs should be replaced. If the plates show wear, then new plates can be tried on their own before resorting to new preload springs. Sometimes it may be found that the slipping torque is higher than specified, especially if new components have been fitted. If the torque is much greater than specified, it could increase the steering effort to an unacceptable level. Some LSD manufacturers supply different-rate preload springs to allow adjustment of slipping torque to suit the vehicle. If different-rate springs are required, they may be available from the differential manufacturer direct, if not available from the car manufacturer.

Chapter 6 | Propshaft, driveshafts and joints

Shafts are employed in the transmission system of a car to transmit the torque between the separate components, e.g. between gearbox and final drive or between final drive and road wheels. In early vehicles, where shafts were used, the drivetrain was laid out so that the components were in exact alignment and straight shafts with rigid fixings to the components could be used. More modern vehicles, for reasons of space efficiency and suspension choice, always use jointed shafts to transmit drive and so allow lateral and angular displacements between components.

While the function of such shafts is simple, there is a great diversity of shaft design, because of the widely varying detail requirements of a particular suspension or engine layout and the great variety of joints available. Shafts for the more popular transmission layouts, e.g. propshafts for front-inline-engined, rear-wheel-drive cars or driveshafts for transverse-engined, front-wheel-drive cars, do, however, display similarity from car to car and so will be discussed in these broad categories.

Propeller shafts

The shaft joining the gearbox output to the final drive input on a Hotchkiss layout rear-wheel-drive car is the propeller shaft or propshaft. On live-axled cars the propshaft must allow both angular misalignment at its two ends and also allow 'plunge', the telescoping of the shaft as the live axle moves forward and backward with suspension deflection. Propshafts are most commonly made of drawn tubular steel and may be a single piece, with a joint at each end, or two-piece with a centre chassis mounting incorporating a bearing and another joint. The joints used

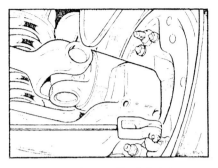

Above **Fig. 6.1. Hooke's joint on a Hillman Imp**

Below **Fig. 6.2. Rubber doughnut joint on the Ford Granada (A—doughnut joint; B—centre bearing; C— Hooke's joints)**

are usually of the single Hooke's type (Fig. 6.1), but occasionally a flexible rubber joint is used such as the rubber doughnut type (Fig. 6.2), as used on many Fords, or the Layrub multiple bush joint. Some older cars used weird and wonderful types such as the flexible strap joint (Fig. 6.3), used on some Triumph Heralds, presumably for economy as this joint has few virtues. Modern cars are increasingly using a Birfield-type joint (Fig. 6.4) in the propshaft, where this joint may accept plunge, but little is made of its constant velocity capability, which is discussed later.

This basic open type of shaft is used on the majority of rear-wheel-drive cars, but mention must be made of the other main type used. This is the 'torque tube' as used on the Peugeot 504/505/604 models, where the only joint is at the gearbox output and the shaft is enclosed in a 'torque tube' which transmits the torque reaction from the final drive back to the power unit. A variation on this is used on some front-engine, rear-gearbox cars, such as the Alfa Romeo, and another variation, the short or semi-torque

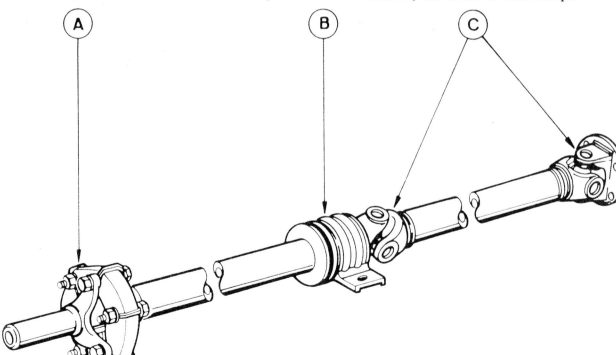

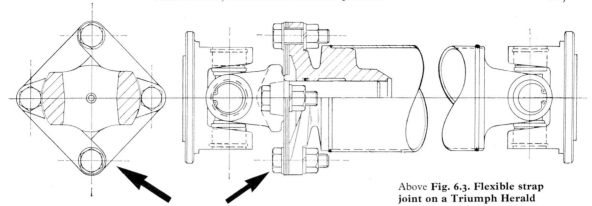

tube, is used on many rear-wheel-drive Vauxhall and Opel models. The torque tube type of shafts have fewer joints and accept less angle change in the joints and so are far less likely to need regular overhaul.

Propshafts, because of their simple function, have few problem areas when overhauling. Common faults include joint wear, centre mounting failure and shaft imbalance. Less likely is bending of or other damage to the shaft, or spline wear. A problem with the propshaft is generally indicated by an unusual noise from the floorpan while travelling, which may range from a low rumble to a heavy thumping if the centre mounting has failed. The propshaft should be inspected if a fault is suspected and certainly before each annual MOT test.

Whatever type of propshaft joint is fitted, it must have minimal play rotationally or laterally if the propshaft is moved by hand with the car out of gear. If a rubber joint is fitted there should be no splits in it or other signs of delamination from the metal drive flanges or tubes. Enclosed lubricated joints should have no splits in or other leakages from their boots. Bearing cups visible on the outside of the cruciform of Hooke's joints should be firmly retained either by a circlip or by 'staking'—punching in of the metal around the cup. The flange bolts or studs securing the joints to the gearbox tailshaft or the final drive input shaft should all be present and tight. If the shaft is two-piece with a centre mounting, the mounting should be firmly secured to the floorpan or chassis and should have no splits in it, if of the flexible rubber type.

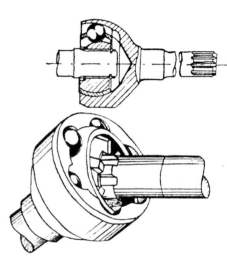

Fig. 6.4. The Hardy Spicer Birfield joint

If none of these checks turns up a fault, but vibration is present, a further check can be made to see whether a balance weight has become detached from the shaft. This can be indicated by a small, particularly clean patch on the shaft, but may not always be visible. The shaft may also be checked by eye for straightness, though even a slight bend would cause terrible vibration.

If a fault is discovered in the shaft this will almost always mean the removal of the shaft from the car for repair. Removal will entail the disconnection of the shaft at both ends and maybe the freeing of the centre mounting from the chassis. The ease of removal is often very good, but some cars have obstructive underbody features, such as the transmission tunnel floor on an MGB. When undoing propshaft joint flanges the two halves of the flange should always be marked so that they may be reassembled in the same orientation to minimize the risk of causing imbalance. With the shaft out of the car the same inspection can be repeated, as there is a good likelihood that a fault has gone unobserved in the darkness underneath the car.

Split flexible rubber joints require replacement with a new item, as do worn enclosed Birfield-type joints. Split boots on the enclosed type of joint may be replaced but, unfortunately, as is often the case nowadays, the joints themselves are usually classed by the manufacturer as non-serviceable items and only complete new joints are available. The Hooke's joint, however, is fully serviceable and the parts to repair them are readily available from Quinton-Hazel and other pattern part manufacturers. A repair kit can be purchased which contains a new cruciform and new bearing cups and, where applicable, retaining circlips. This is to be preferred to replacing only some components of the joint, even if they are available individually, as any worn components left in place will mean that the shaft must be removed sooner for the next overhaul. If circlips are not used and the cups are staked in, the deformed metal around the cup must be removed by careful grinding, chiselling or drilling to free the cup. When the cups have been freed they are removed from their holders by pressing or hammering the opposite cup inwards (Fig. 6.5). A vice to support the shaft is very useful here. The cups are not always easy to drift out and care must be taken not to damage the housings, as this may result in the new cup being impossible to insert or being too loose. When the housings have been cleaned and deburred, the new cups are drifted into place. Don't forget to put the cruciform in the centre before doing this, as you will only have to start again otherwise! The cups are secured by replacing the circlips or restaking the edge of the housing around the cup with a staking punch or any suitable, preferably square, punch.

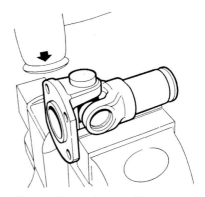

Fig. 6.5. Removing cruciform from Hooke's joint

The centre bearing/mounting is also usually a non-serviceable item. Replacement of this may require the separation of the two halves of the propshaft to free the bearing.

A sliding splined coupling is often used to transfer the drive either from the gearbox or to the final drive and accept the propshaft plunge. The sliding splines rarely wear to a great degree, but, if excessive play is found, should be inspected further. The splines should not have any visible wear ridges along their sides or on their tops. If spline wear is found to be causing vibration, the only solution is replacement of the components. The splines may be lightly lubricated with a metallized anti-fretting grease, such as Copaslip, before reassembly.

If vibration has been isolated to propshaft imbalance, providing the shaft is not bent, it is often possible to purchase a balanced exchange shaft from a motor factor. These exchange shafts have usually also had the joints overhauled and so can be an expensive cure for simple imbalance. A bent propshaft should be replaced with a new one as there is little that can easily be done to straighten it. If a new shaft is not available, for a classic car for example, the owners club for the marque can often put you in touch with a source of supply.

Replacement of the propshaft, as all the best manuals say, is simply the reverse of removal, taking care to align the joint flanges in their previous positions.

Driveshafts

The main difference in the function of driveshafts,

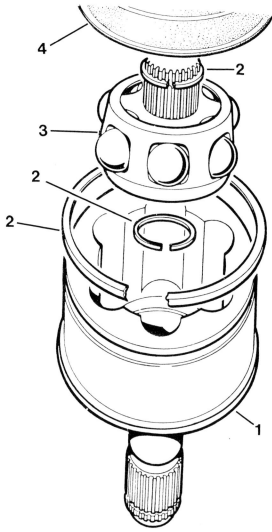

Fig. 6.6. Allegro plunging inner joint (1—joint outer at differential end; 2—retainers; 3—cage and balls on inner hub; 4—gaiter)

compared to propshafts, is the accommodation of far greater and more frequent angular and plunge movements. This difference is reflected in a different choice of joint, particularly on front-wheel-drive cars, where steering also adds to outer joint angular movement. Deflecting driveshafts are found on all front-wheel-drive cars and also on rear-wheel-drive cars with independent suspension or a de Dion dead tube axle. In these cases there is always the requirement to transmit the drive from a chassis- or gearbox-mounted final drive to the driven wheels, which are deflecting with the suspension.

Driveshafts on front-wheel-drive cars, particularly modern ones, tend to be of similar design. The shaft is usually one-piece steel with a constant velocity outer joint and an enclosed, plunging inner joint (Fig. 6.6). On more powerful front-wheel-drive cars the designer often tries to use equal-length driveshafts in order to avoid the problem of torque-steer and, in the case of a transverse-engined car, this may mean the addition of a support bearing and inboard joint opposite the offset differential (Fig. 6.7).

Most rear-wheel-drive, independent suspension cars use a similar design of shaft with the exception of the joints, which are rarely of the constant velocity type. Older cars of this type used Hooke's joints at both ends of the shaft, but as with propshafts, enclosed-type joints are now fitted more and more often, as on the Ford Sierra and Granada models (Fig. 6.8).

Before dealing with the overhaul of driveshafts it is worthwhile looking at the many different types of joints used, which, though different in detail, really only consist of four main types.

The first type, which has already been mentioned in the section on propshafts, is the Hooke's joint. The Hooke's joints used on driveshafts are very similar to those used on

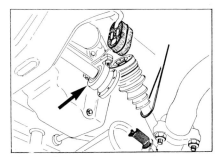

Fig. 6.7. Support bearing on Fiesta 1.6 equal-length driveshaft

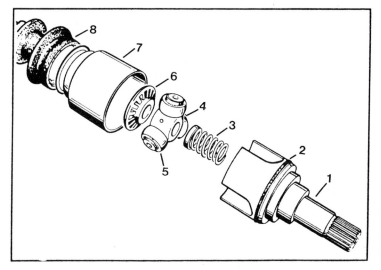

Fig. 6.8. Sierra enclosed tripodal driveshaft joint (1—joint input and slider; 2—outer body grease seal; 3—compression spring; 4—inner hub or 'spider'; 5—rolling sphere; 6—retainer; 7—outer body; 8—gaiter)

**Fig. 6.9. Double Hooke's-type
outer joint on the Renault 16**

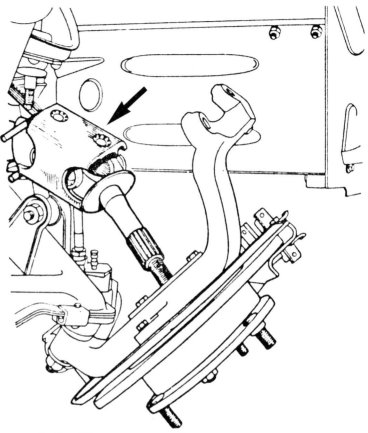

propshafts. They are most often fitted singly to either end
of a rear-wheel-drive driveshaft, but, occasionally, are
fitted in twos at the outer end of a front-wheel-drive
driveshaft, where the fitting of a pair in the correct angular
relationship to each other effectively produces a constant
velocity joint (Fig. 6.9).

The second type has until now been referred to as a
Birfield-type joint, but is really a family of very similar
joints. The original joint was designed by a Hungarian
called Rzeppa for use in submarine conning towers and
patented in America in 1935. The modern version is
manufactured by Hardy Spicer and is called the Birfield
joint, though it still retains the basic six ball and cage
arrangement of the original (Fig. 6.10). The principal
feature of this type of joint is that it is a 'constant velocity'

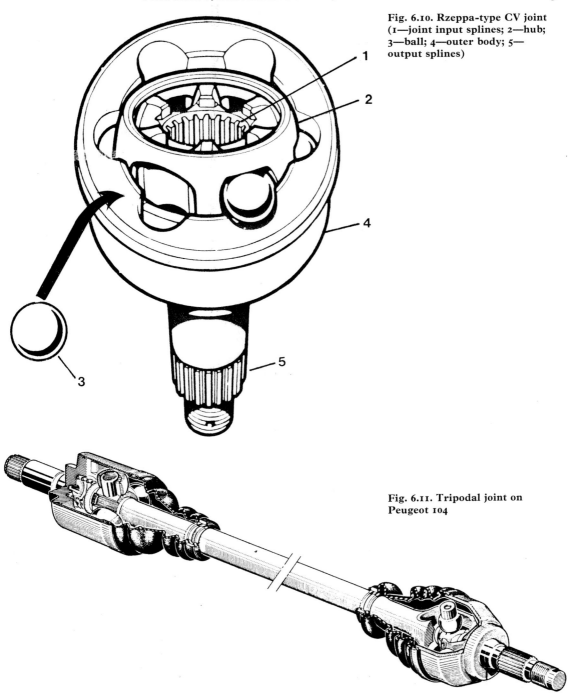

Fig. 6.10. Rzeppa-type CV joint (1—joint input splines; 2—hub; 3—ball; 4—outer body; 5—output splines)

Fig. 6.11. Tripodal joint on Peugeot 104

joint, which literally means that the velocity of the output side is always the same as that of the input side, irrespective of the angular deflection in the joint. This feature is particularly important in the outer joints of front-wheel-drive driveshafts, where the use of a non-constant velocity joint produces an unpleasant shuddering in the drivetrain during tight corners as the wheels try to accelerate and decelerate during each revolution. The basic design of this joint does not accept plunge, but modern versions exist which do.

A third type of joint, which looks outwardly like the Birfield type, is the bipodal or tripodal type (Fig. 6.11). This type of joint is used on Sierras and modern French rear-wheel-drive driveshafts and at the inner end of front-wheel-drive driveshafts. The bipodal or tripodal type is not a constant velocity joint and so has a more limited application, but has the benefits of accepting plunge, being cheap to manufacture and being robust.

The fourth broad group is flexible couplings, which were used on older rear-wheel-drive cars and at the inner end of front-wheel-drive driveshafts. These include the doughnut and Austin cruciform designs (Fig. 6.12), but this type is used less often now due to short life expectancy.

Faults in driveshafts are almost invariably due to joint wear which is indicated by vibration or knocking on rear-wheel-drive cars. Faults in front-wheel-drive driveshafts are usually due to the outer joint, which wears a lot faster than the inner, and is indicated by a rumble or knock while turning sharp corners. Where bipodal or tripodal jointed shafts are used in front-wheel-drive applications, worn joints often produce an out-of-balance shaking, which manifests itself throughout the car and alters as the accelerator is depressed and released. If a Birfield-type joint is fitted then a 'pinging' sound may also be heard during cornering as the balls are shot about inside the joint.

An inspection of driveshafts should include checking for excessive lateral or rotational play in the joints, as with the propshaft, and particular attention should be paid to checking the boots of enclosed Birfield, bipodal and tripodal joints for splits. Splits allow the leakage of lubricant and the ingress of abrasive dirt, which causes rapid deterioration of the joint. Splits are not repairable, and if any are found the driveshaft should be removed for the fitment of a new boot and inspection of the inside of the joint for damage. Hooke's and rubber joints should be examined as described in the propshaft section.

On most cars no work can be carried out on the driveshaft without its removal from the car. The removal procedure depends on the particular suspension design used and on front-wheel-drive cars it typically requires the freeing of the hub carrier or track control arm for shaft withdrawal.

If an apparently redundant weight is found fitted to a front-wheel-drive driveshaft, usually to the longer of the pair, this is a torsional damper weight and is used to 'tune' the shaft to avoid torsional shuddering. Damper weights, if removed, must be replaced in the same position on the shaft so this position should be marked during disassembly.

With the shaft on the bench the joints may be removed. With Hooke's joints, follow the procedure described in the propshaft section. Flexible joints are simply unbolted and replaced, though some types, e.g. the doughnut type fitted to the Hillman Imp (Fig. 6.13), require radial precompression with a special tool or large jubilee clip. This requirement will be obvious, as the joint will appear not to fit in its uncompressed state.

With Birfield, bipodal and tripodal joints the boot must be freed by removal or cutting of its retaining straps and slid up the shaft before joint removal. Some enclosed joints, such as the Glaenzer-Spicer tripodal joints used by Peugeot, have a thin steel canister around the joint, which must be removed, in addition to the boot, by peening the edges back, before the joint can be dismantled. The plunging type of Birfield joint will separate by hand into two parts for inspection, but the non-plunging type requires the removal of the shaft before dismantling. The shaft is usually retained in the joint by means of an internal spring circlip and is removed by knocking the joint from the shaft with a hide mallet, while holding the shaft in a vice. When removed, the cage of the joint is rotated to free the balls one by one until the case can be removed. Bipodal

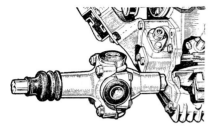

Fig. 6.12. Austin flexible cruciform driveshaft joint

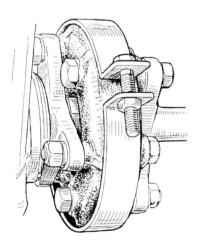

Fig. 6.13. Precompressing a rubber doughnut joint with a strap

and tripodal joints will also separate by hand without shaft removal, but be careful not to lose the internal compression spring sometimes fitted.

It is worthwhile at this stage to look at the condition of the grease within the joint. If the grease is too sparse or contains abrasive particles this is a strong indication that damage will be found. With the joints in pieces the surface of the components can be inspected for wear. The contact surfaces of all the joint components should be smooth and free from pits, but polishing of the surfaces is normal and should not be confused with wear. The contact surfaces include the balls, centre piece and outer of the Birfield joint and the part-spherical rollers and outer of bipodal and tripodal types (Fig. 6.14). Any pitting indicates that the joint should be renewed, as further wear is accelerated. Replacement joints of the Birfield and bipodal or tripodal types are usually supplied as complete units with a new boot and suitable grease. The grease used is usually a molybdenum-disulphate-filled lithium grease, but manufacturers generally recommend their own brand of grease, which should be obtained, if not supplied with the new joint.

Reassembly of the Birfield-type joint is the reverse of dismantling, but bipodal and tripodal types also require the removal of the centre piece from the shaft and its replacement with the new piece. The centre pieces of bipodal or tripodal joints, if fitted to both ends of a shaft, must be replaced in the correct angular position relative to each other to avoid shuddering in operation. The correct position should be obtained from the workshop manual. When the joint has been reassembled on the shaft, the boot, suitably packed with grease, may be replaced. Replacing the boot can be very frustrating and difficult for one person, but enlisting some help and supporting the shaft in a vice will ease the task. The air trapped in the boot must be bled by compressing the boot, as this can expand when the joint heats up in use and cause ballooning and fretting.

If the boot-retaining clips are undamaged they may be reused, but often it is safer to replace used clips with electrical cable ties, which are a good substitute. Be careful when tightening clips or ties that the boot is not pierced by

Fig. 6.14. Removing central spider of tripodal joint: (1) rollers retained with tape; (2) circlip pliers used to free spider. Wear areas: (3) roller surfaces; (4) roller channels

overtightening and that no sharp edges are left in contact with the boot.

Before replacing the shaft, check that the joint rotates freely and that the boot folds properly as the joint is rotated. Some bipodal and tripodal joints need to be held compressed on to the shaft during replacement by stiff wire or cord to prevent the internal spring forcing the joint apart. Care should also be taken not to catch the boots on the chassis or other parts, which could puncture the boots.

Chapter 7 | Gearchanges and linkages

This chapter has to remain fairly general in nature due to the literally hundreds of different types of gearchange linkage in existence.

With gearchanges and linkages we are concerned with the mechanisms which control the internal selectors of the gearbox, i.e. everything from the gear lever to the gearbox casing. The many different types of gearchange mechanism all have a common purpose—to translate the driver's positioning of the gear lever into selection of the correct gears within the gearbox and to do so remotely. Some gearchange linkage layouts are remarkably simple: a three-speed-plus-reverse gearbox mounted inline with the car and positioned between the front seats will probably have a mechanism many times less complex than a five-speed-plus-reverse gearbox mounted transversely at the rear of the car. The complexity of the gearchange linkage is most often determined by the orientation of the gearbox rather than any other factor excepting, of course, complexity necessitated by the avoidance of components of the car which are positioned in the ideal path of the linkage.

Where a gearbox is mounted inline with the car, the to-and-fro movements of gear selection at the lever correspond directly to movement of the synchronizer assemblies in the same plane, so the design of gearchange can be straightforward. With transverse installations, however, lever movement is at right-angles to synchronizer movement, so means by which to change the direction of movement must be incorporated into the gearchange system. Naturally this requires more components such as universal joints, rubber couplings and bell-cranks and often this results in extra friction and imprecision—especially when wear and/or seizure have occurred.

Essentially, the restoration of gearchange mechanisms involves the elimination of excessive wear in joints, bushes and guides and excessive stiffness in any moving parts. Some cars, such as the front-wheel-drive Ford Fiesta/ Escort and the Vauxhall Nova/Astra/Cavalier, have a gearchange mechanism which requires precise angular alignment (Fig. 7.1) on assembly or reconnection if difficult or impossible gear selection is to be avoided; again, we must stress the importance of workshop manuals to back up even what appears to be the simplest task.

Other cars (and here French cars are most notable) have tubular gearchange rods comprising snap-fit ball and socket joints at their ends. Such rods are often screw-adjustable for length (Fig. 7.2), and if the specified length measurements are not adhered to when installing new rods or screwing new joints on to them, then problems will invariably be experienced with gear selection. Incidentally, the sockets of the ball joints on this type are usually nylon lined and if they are not kept lightly greased they can seize solid and the nylon can disintegrate. A bell-crank lever can be found on some transverse gearbox linkages (A, Figs. 7.3 and 7.5); this is simply a pivoting 'L'-shaped lever which translates fore-and-aft motion into lateral motion. If the post on which it pivots is worn then expect a sloppy gear lever action.

A fairly substantial spring found attached to an external gear linkage is usually a gate-bias spring which automatically pulls the gear lever into the third/fourth plane when neutral is selected (B, Fig. 7.3). This aids the speed of gearchange when 'going up' the gearbox and is often fitted so that the driver doesn't get into the habit of forcing the lever too far to the right when aiming for third gear, and ending up in reverse. On front-wheel-drive Fords especially, this spring looks like a DIY afterthought and many people have been known to leave it off—which doesn't help matters at all.

Some older cars (such as early Austin Maxis) employ cables known as bowden cables for the gearchange linkages, rather than rods (Fig. 7.4). These have the

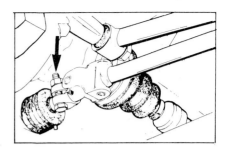

Above **Fig. 7.1.** This Ford Fiesta/Escort gearchange clamp coupling requires precise angular alignment if satisfactory gearchange action is to be obtained; a positioning tool is used to guarantee correct alignment

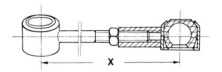

Above **Fig. 7.2.** A shortened illustration of an adjustable gearchange rod with snap-fit ball joints at its ends. Only the right-hand joint is screw adjustable for length; the locknut at the centre secures its position. The distance 'X' between ball joint centres is critical

Fig. 7.3. This frighteningly complex gearchange mechanism belongs to a front-wheel-drive car with a transverse gearbox. The bellcrank lever (A) translates side-to-side movement (of the lever between first/second and third/fourth planes) into fore-and-aft movement into the gearbox. The spring shown at 'B' is a gate- (plane-) bias spring which keeps the gear lever in the third/fourth plane

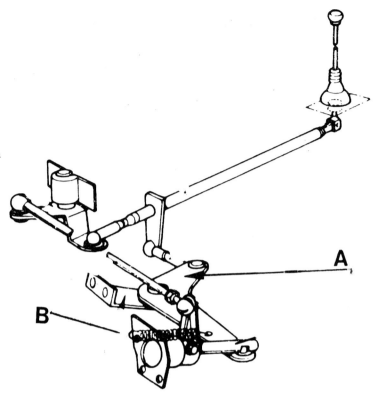

advantage of being flexible, so simplifying the mechanism by eliminating the need for joints. They also tend to be more troublesome in the long run as they can stretch and they require frequent lubrication. With cables, length adjustment is critical and, due to the tendency for stretching, it often has to be put into practice. Another use for cables in gearchanges is for the *reverse lock*, a frequently used device which prevents accidental selection of reverse. With a reverse lock you must raise the gear lever (or a part of it) before the movement required for the selection of reverse gear can be made. The rear-wheel-drive General Motors Cavalier/Ascona/Manta series employs a cable inside the gear lever which is pulled up by a finger plate just under the lever knob; breakage of this cable will prevent any selection of reverse gear whatsoever. While on the subject of gear lever *knobs*, it is worth mentioning that

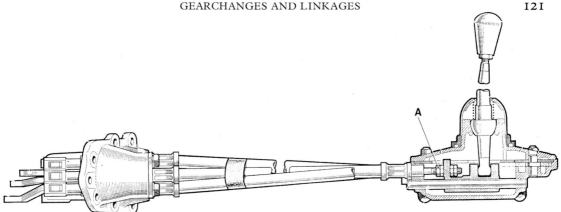

where there is no apparent fastening for the knob on to the lever, it is usually either screwed on or an interference-fit on the lever, in which case it can only be removed by immersing it in very hot water to expand it.

The inspection and repair of gearchange linkages requires basic common sense as they are invariably 'common sense' systems of which the operation can always be easily traced by eye. Wear (excess free play) and stiffness are the two main enemies to good gearchange operation and the fundamental rules are that metal joints (i.e. moving joints such as universal joints) should be kept lubricated as specified, plastic or rubber bushes should not be split, perished or flabby due to oil contamination, and linkage lengths, where adjustable, should be correct. Where two shafts are splined or clamped together, there is usually only one correct angular relationship between the two for guaranteeing satisfactory gear selection, so always refer to the relevant workshop manual before just 'bolting together'. If the two shaft ends are splined then there may be a thicker 'master' spline on each to indicate alignment.

Above **Fig. 7.4. The cable-type gearchange from an early front-wheel-drive Austin. The adjustment and locknuts are shown at A**

Below **Fig. 7.5. The gearchange mechanism of the front-wheel-drive Peugeot 104, also showing the selector rails and forks inside the gearbox. At 'A' can be seen a bellcrank lever while 'B' is a fine example of a fixed-length steady rod**

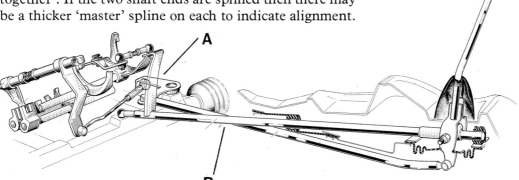

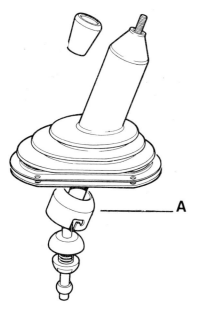

A

Fig. 7.6. The bayonet ball-joint cup at 'A' (in this case a Mini/Allegro type) is a typical method of gear lever retention—the joint should be kept copiously greased. Many Ford rear-wheel-drive inline gearboxes have a similar joint where the joint cup is made from nylon and screws down on to the lever ball

The gearchange *steady rod* (B, Fig. 7.5), which is common on front-wheel-drive cars, has a very important task: although appearing to be an inert rod or bar bolted between gear lever mounting and gearbox and not actually an operational part of the change mechanism, it maintains a constant distance between the car's power unit and the gear lever so that as the engine rocks and the gearbox effectively moves towards and away from the driver, the gear lever moves with it. This guarantees that the distances and angles calculated in the design of the external gearchange mechanism are kept constant with gearbox movement so that gearchange alignment is assured at all times. If the steady rod has rubber bushes at one or both ends then it is important that these are in good condition; similarly, if the rod is of the adjustable type then it must be kept at the specified overall length.

Almost every type of fixing and fastening is used on gearchange linkages but the common ones are: roll pins (spring-steel tubes with a slot along their length), clevis pins (simple steel through-pins) secured by split pins, spring clips or circlips, clamps (with pinch bolts), internal and external circlips, bayonet cups (found at the base of many gear levers such as the Leyland 'gears-in-sump' gearchange, Fig. 7.6, and unfastened like a light bulb), and of course, the conventional nut and bolt.

So there should be no mystery attached to any gearchange mechanism, least of all on conventional front-engine, rear-wheel-drive cars where the linkage is short and direct. As long as unwanted 'slop' is eliminated from moving parts, grease is used where necessary, stiffness is eliminated by cleaning and lubricating, and lengths and angular relationships are maintained as specified, the proper functioning of the gearbox synchromesh should be guaranteed.

One final point worth noting is that a buzzing gear lever is invariably induced either by looseness in the system or insufficient grease at its base. If it is of the enclosed ball-joint type at its bottom end, generous packing of this joint with multi-purpose grease is beneficial and will dampen out annoying vibration.

Troubleshooter

PROBLEM	POSSIBLE CAUSE	CURE
Clutch slips	Friction plate worn	Renew friction plate
	Release mechanism out of adjustment	Adjust mechanism
	Oil or grease on friction surfaces	Clean surfaces/renew friction plate
	Weak coil springs or diaphragm	Renew springs or diaphragm (cover)
Clutch drags (stiff gearchange, 'crunching' on reverse engagement)	Too much free play in release mechanism	Adjust mechanism/renew clutch cable
	Carpet/mats limiting pedal travel	Remove restriction
	Leaking hydraulic release mechanism	Locate and rectify leak
	Worn friction plate	Renew friction plate
	Friction plate sticking on splines	Clean/deburr splines
Clutch judders	Loose/worn engine/ gearbox mountings	Tighten/renew mountings
	Oil contamination of friction surfaces	Clean surfaces/renew friction plate
	Distorted friction surfaces	Locate distorted component(s) and renew

Rattle from clutch housing when pedal released	Normal condition on many cars	
	Worn release bearing	Renew bearing
	Inadequately greased release lever pivots	Grease as required
	Inadequately secured release bearing (where fitted with retainer)	Secure bearing
Screeching from clutch housing when disengaging clutch	Worn release bearing	Renew bearing
Oil leak(s) from gearbox	Worn oil seal(s), distorted casing(s)/cover(s) or damaged gasket(s)	Locate source, check fo casing/cover looseness (distortion, replace gasket(s)/seal(s)
'Crunching' gear engagement (one or more gears)	Normal condition on some cars when cold	
	Gearbox oil too thick	Drain/refill with correct grade
	Worn/incorrectly adjusted clutch	Renew/adjust clutch
	Worn synchromesh cone clutch(es)	Overhaul gearbox
	Weak synchromesh or selector detent springs	Renew springs
	Excessive gear wheel or mainshaft endfloat	Overhaul gearbox
Stiff gearchange	Normal condition on some cars when cold	
	Gearbox oil too thick	Drain/refill with correct grade
	Gearchange linkage out of alignment (where applicable)	Align linkage
	Gearchange linkage joint/bearing seizure	Locate and rectify

Loss of one or more gears	Broken gearchange linkage, broken or loose selector fork(s)	Check/rectify linkage or tighten/renew fork(s)
Jumping out of one or more gears	Loose/worn engine/ gearbox mountings Worn/broken selector/ synchronizer detent spring(s) Badly worn synchronizer dog teeth	Tighten/renew mountings Renew spring(s) Overhaul gearbox
Continual whining or droning from gearbox	Worn gear wheels/shaft bearings or excessive shaft endfloat	Overhaul gearbox
Regular 'clicking' from gearbox	Chipped or broken gear wheel tooth	Overhaul gearbox
Overdrive does not engage	Defect in electric actuation circuit Insufficient oil in overdrive Malfunction in inhibitor switch Blocked overdrive oil filter	Trace fault and rectify Top-up with oil Check and repair/renew switch Clean filter
'Clunk' in transmission when pulling away or on overrun	Worn propshaft joint(s)/ spline(s) Excessive backlash in final drive Worn axle shaft joints/ splines	Renew joint(s) or propshaft Overhaul/renew final drive Renew joints or shafts
Rumbling/vibration from region of floorpan when decelerating	Worn propshaft centre bearing	Renew bearing
Shuddering from region of floorpan	Out of balance or bent propshaft	Balance/renew propshaft

Knocking or 'pinging' noise when cornering (fwd only)	Worn driveshaft outer joints	Overhaul or renew join
Knocking from engine compartment (fwd only)	Loose unequal-length driveshaft support bearing mounting	Tighten bearing mounting
Constant droning noise from rear of car (rwd only)	Worn final drive bearings	Overhaul final drive
Whining noise from rear of car (rwd only)	Worn final drive bearings or pinion and crown wheel	Overhaul final drive
Rumbling noise from differential when cornering	Worn differential components	Overhaul differential
Excessive wheelspin in low traction conditions (LSD only)	Worn LSD clutch components or weak preload springs	Overhaul LSD or rene preload springs
Excessive steering effort at low speeds (LSD only)	LSD preload springs too strong	Change LSD preload springs

Index

A
Alfa Romeo SpA 8, 40, 106
  Alfetta 40, 41, 42
  Giulietta 40
  GTV 40
asbestos 14, 60
Austin 44, 46, 121
  Allegro 22, 110, 122
  Maestro 95
  Maxi 119
  Metro 22
  Mini 22, 29, 42, 44, 45, 46, 48,
    59, 60, 62, 66, 73, 77, 90, 122
  Montego 35
Austin Rover Group Ltd
  (Leyland) 8
Autodata Ltd 7, 10
Automotive Products PLC 8
axle
  de Dion 40, 110
  live 32

B
ball-race bearings 10, 56
basic tool kit 10
baulk ring 25, 26, 27, 30
bipodal joint (see joints)
Birfield-type constant velocity joint
  (see joints)
blocker bars 26, 27, 28, 29
Borg & Beck 66
bowden cable 119
Buick 28, 82, 88

C
Chrysler Avenger 54
clutch 14, 53
  cone 23, 24, 53
  dog 22, 23
  drag 59, 61
  friction 53
  riding 61
Copaslip 60, 109
couplings
  Austin cruciform 114, 116
  doughnut 114, 116
  flexible 114
crash-box 21
crown wheel 13, 16, 37

D
DAF 94
Datsun Cherry 28
dial gauge 90
dial test indicator 99
differential 16
dog-tooth set 27
double-declutching 19, 21, 23, 24
doughnut joint 114, 116

E
endfloat 90
Eurobox 46

F
Ferguson 102
Fiat 48
final drive 13, 16
flexible couplings 114
flexible strap joint 106
Ford Motor Co. Ltd 8, 19
Ford 27, 29, 48, 59, 122
  Cortina 58
  Escort 89, 119
  Fiesta 59, 111, 119
  Granada 106, 111
  GT40 38
  Sierra 35, 91, 95, 99, 111, 114
four-wheel drive 50
Frazer Nash 31
friction clutch 14
friction plate 14, 15

G
G-clamp 69
gearbox
  constant-mesh 21
  overhaul 68
  sliding-mesh 17, 18, 21, 22
General Motors 27, 29, 59
  Ascona 120
  Cavalier 120
  Manta 120
Getrag gearbox 71, 73, 74, 81, 83
Glaenzer-Spicer tripodal joints 115
Gunk 10

H
Hammerite 89
Hardy Spicer Birfield joint 107, 112

Hewland 39
Hillier & Pittuck 8
Hillman Imp 106, 115
Honda 83
Hooke's joints 36, 52, 106, 107, 108,
  109, 111, 112, 115
Hotchkiss 33, 105
Hutchinson & Co. Ltd 7

I
Issigonis, Sir Alec 42

J
Jaguar Cars Ltd 8
Jaguar Mk 2 32, 33, 71
Jensen FF 102
joints
  bipodal 114, 115, 116
  Birfield 42, 50, 106, 108, 112,
    114, 115, 116
  flexible strap 106
  Glaenzer-Spicer tripodal 115
  Hardy Spicer Birfield 107, 112
  Hooke's 36, 52, 106, 107, 108,
    109, 111, 112, 115
  Layrub multiple bush 106
  Rzeppa 45, 112, 113
  tripodal 47, 113, 114, 115, 116,
    117

L
Land Rover 50, 52
Laycock de Normanville overdrive
  unit 33, 34
layshaft 17, 18, 20
Leyland 27, 28, 29, 60, 73, 77, 84,
  122
  Mini (see Austin)
limited slip differential 101, 102
lithium grease 116
Loctite 81, 84

M
methylated spirit 89
MGB 108
molybdenum disulphide 116
Morris Minor 54, 55
MOT test 107

O
Opel 107
O-rings 71, 92
overdrive 12, 32, 34

P
Panhard rod 33
Peugeot Société Anonyme 8
Peugeot 27, 28, 48, 57, 63, 66, 82,
    87, 88, 115
    104 113, 121
    204/304 79
    305 72, 73, 74, 76, 79, 93
    404 94, 95, 96, 101
    504/505/604 106
pinch distance 99
pinion 13
planet gears 16, 34
Porsche 37, 40, 41
Porsche, Dr Ferdinand 38
preload 89, 90, 99
proportional load synchromesh 25

Q
Quinton-Hazel 108

R
Rawlbolt 68

Red Hermetite 93
Regie Nationale Des Usines
    Renault 8
Renault 42, 48
    Dauphine 37
    5 46, 47, 50, 71, 75, 92
    16 112
    18 71, 75, 93, 99
reverse lock 120
Rzeppa 112
    constant velocity joints 45
    CV joint 113

S
Saab 31, 42
selector mechanisms 72
semi-torque tube 106
silicone rubber 89
sliding-mesh gearbox (see gearbox)
solenoid valve 34
staking 107
Stanley knife 89
steady rod 122
sun gear 16, 34
synchromesh 17, 23
    proportional load 25
synchronizer hub 24

T
thermochromatic pencil 85
Thornton Powr-Lok limited slip
    differential (LSD) 35, 101, 103
torque tube 106
transaxle 37, 38, 39
transfer box 50
transmission layouts 31
    principles 11
tripodal joints (see joints)
Triumph
    Acclaim 83
    Herald 106, 107

V
V.A.G. Ltd. 8
Vauxhall 48, 49, 107
    Astra 48, 49, 74, 90, 119
    Carlton 71
    Cavalier 35, 90, 119
    Nova 90, 119
Volkswagen
    Beetle 37, 38, 39, 77, 84
    Golf 57, 84, 91
    Polo 84
    Variant 37
Volvo 40